ALIVE TO GOD THROUGH PRAISE

ALIVE TO GOD THROUGH PRAISE

EDITED AND PARAPHRASED BY
DONALD E. DEMARAY

Wipf & Stock
PUBLISHERS
Eugene, Oregon

Wipf and Stock Publishers
199 W 8th Ave, Suite 3
Eugene, OR 97401

Alive To God Through Praise
Edited by Demaray, Donald E.
Copyright©1976 by Demaray, Donald E.
ISBN: 1-59752-809-9
Publication date 7/5/2006
Previously published by Baker Book House Company, 1976

To
the memory of
ROBERT M. FINE
whose very life was praise

ACKNOWLEDGMENTS

It is my pleasure to extend warm thanks to those who, in one way or another, have made possible this guide to praise.

To the Officers of Administration, Asbury Theological Seminary, go thanks for sabbatical leave, the summer of 1975, to work on fresh and contemporary renderings of material from the Christian classics.

Further thanks must be expressed to the gracious people at the University of Durham Library in Durham, England, where I was made to feel perfectly at home. Also in Durham, The Reverend and Mrs. Anthony Casurella, and The Reverend and Mrs. Robert Gordon helped in many ways.

In the Manchester, England, area, I must thank Mr. and Mrs. John Bowie for many courtesies and kindnesses; and to the Manchester Public Library and the Timperley Public Library go further thanks.

Three pastors and their churches in Lancashire, England, which have learned the secrets of divine praise, provided a backdrop of inspiration I shall long remember. The ministers are The Reverend Frank Mitchell of Morcambe, The Reverend Barrie Walton of Garstang, and The Reverend Ronald Taylor of Wiggan. Skip and Linda Ball of Morcambe, and Alan and Mary Ramm of Garstang extended courtesies which I dare not overlook and for which I am deeply grateful.

In Northern Ireland I found both leisure and inspiration for forwarding this little volume; thanks for the kindnesses of The Reverend and Mrs. Victor Trinder, and The Reverend and Mrs. John Hutchinson of Belfast. Mr. Trinder opened the door to ten days on the Isle of Man, where the final typing of the manuscript was done.

Dr. Thomas A. Carruth of Wilmore, Kentucky, and Mr. Robert M. Welch of Irvine, Kentucky, made beautiful contributions to making possible this volume.

The Reverend Robert F. Andrews, Winona Lake, Indiana, the head of the outreach and evangelism work of the Free Methodist Church of North America, has been most cooperative, and I must thank him warmly.

Dr. Susan Schultz, Director of Library Services, Asbury Theological Seminary, is always kind, cooperative and genuinely helpful.

The Bodlein Library, Oxford University, kindly made available their facilities, and study in that lovely old place doubled the joy of research.

For the encouragement and inspiration of my family— Kathleen my good wife, my children Cherith and Paul, Elyse and Tom, James— I am deeply grateful. They are my teachers in the life of praise.

I wish to thank the following publishers for allowing me to transpose copyrighted materials into my own format:

> Christian Publications, Inc., for permission to use one paragraph from pp. 7-8 of *God's Greatest Gift to Man* by A. W. Tozer.
>
> Baker Book House for the use of J. D. Robertson's prayer, p. 22 of the *Minister's Worship Handbook.*
>
> Fleming H. Revell for materials from pp. 26-27, 44, 45, 112, and 114-15 of Andrew Murray's *With Christ in the School of Prayer.*
>
> The Macmillan Company for material on p. 68 of William Temple's *Readings in St. John's Gospel.*
>
> Abingdon Press, for Saturday in Week 13, Tuesday in Week 11, and Sunday in Week 13 (exclusive of prayers in the last two) of E. Stanley Jones, *Abundant Living.*

PREFACE

2006 printing of *Alive to God Through Praise*

"Praise opens the door to more grace," said an insightful observer of the spiritual life. No wonder the psalmist lifted his eyes to the hills in praise of God. He knew exactly where his help came from—"My help comes from the Lord, who made heaven and earth" (Psalm 121:1-2, RSV).

I thank God for His gifts of praise and grace. I need them! God makes His people positive thinkers and doers to counteract the bombardment of negatives that surround us. In the grace of praise I've found it!—spiritual reality and the secret of life exuberant, enthusiastic, and affirming

George Herbert, the English pastor and poet, wrote these engaging lines:

> "Thou that hast given so much to me,
> Give one thing more—a grateful heart;
> Not thankful when it pleaseth me,
> As if Thy blessings had spare days;
> But such a heart, whose pulse may be
> Thy praise."

God inhabits the praises of His people (Psalm 22:3, KJV).

Donald E. Demaray
Summer 2006

PREFACE

"We find more exhortations in the Bible to praise God than we find to pray to Him!" Mauree Johnson points this out with almost startling revelation. Praise is, of course, one form of prayer, but puzzling indeed is the comparatively small amount of actual praise material in the devotional guides of our time. One does not look in vain, but almost.

Just outside my library cubicle are the rising towers of centuries-old Durham Cathedral. I cannot walk by that architectural masterpiece without experiencing a sense of awe. My eyes inevitably move skyward, my heart follows, and I find myself in the presence of God.

The towers, steeples, and spires of medieval cathedrals and churches were designed, engineered, and built as expressions of praise. The builders may have been more biblical than they knew! The Bible is filled with praise to Eternal God. The Psalms, hymnbook of the Israelitish nation, and the burst of song which appears with almost calculated regularity throughout, characterize the Word of God.

Why, then, the preoccupation with man, his problems, and his world? Even our modern devotions tend to be man-centered. Surely this is but one more symptom of what Archbishop William Temple called "our self-centeredness which is our original sin."

True, we must tackle our problems. Yes, we must grapple with a bad world in the attempt to cure its ills. All that is part of the challenge of life that stimulates us to attempt progress. But surely we have tackled and grappled so long and seriously that we are frequently in danger of losing our perspective. And, in fact, we often do just that.

How, then, do we maintain our balance? our sense of humor? *One of the doxologies of the Church contains the phrase, "Him praise with mirth!"*

How do we handle our psychological maladies?
What a day when psychiatry learns the therapy of praise!
How do we do our praying?
All petition and no praise makes a dull pray-er, dull even to himself.
How do we handle personal hang-ups?

"To recall God's mercies and faithfulness will save one from debilitating indulgence of worry," says Mauree Johnson.

How can we get our attitudes whole and healthy?

It was also Mrs. Johnson who told of the old mountaineer who said, "When I give thanks it happifies my soul."

Praise is clearly one grand secret of the life more abundant which Jesus promised. (Latin for *abundant,* interestingly enough, translates "wave after wave"!)

By the way, mere superficial praise will not suffice. That may do for a while, even make us feel better momentarily. But in the long view the gratitude of our hearts must tap sources at artesian well depth.

What are those sources? In their written form, they take their cue from the Christian classics. The Bible is, of course, the first and foremost of the classics; thus, the many and varied uses of the Scriptures in this devotional guide. After the Bible come the saints past and present, from St. Augustine to A. W. Tozer. But we deal mostly with saints past because we are living too close to the contemporary saints to pick them out with much confidence.

To assist in the sometimes difficult business of understanding the classical devotions, I have in most cases "translated" archaic and obscure language into "immediate" English, and altered conventional forms to contemporary format.

Each devotional unit is organized after this threefold pattern:

Praise from prophet (Scripture)
Praise by pen (devotional writer)
Praise through prayer (devotional source, sometimes the Bible)

No attempt has been made at strict segregation of materials since Scripture, reading, and prayer overlap. The three categories are made only for convenience and manageability.

One final word. Praise is the essence of worship. The earliest Christian worship was essentially praise-oriented. Later, when Christians became "fixed" in their faith, the center of worship changed to a plea for salvation. Pity! Praise maintains freedom; concentration on needs inevitably brings those frustrations that cry, "Answers elude me." But live in the spirit of praise and see how naturally life flows. Does this profound fact begin to interpret that remarkable verse 3 of Psalm 22 where the Bible text says God is "enthroned on the praises of Israel"?

Donald E. Demaray
Durham, England

CONTENTS

PART ONE: IN PRAISE OF THE GOD WHO LOVES ME 15

Chapter One: Jesus Is My Friend 17
- 1 He Is My Friend! (1) 19
- 2 He Is My Friend! (2) 20
- 3 He Is My Friend! (3) 22
- 4 Praise for Who My Friend Is 24
- 5 Christ Is with Me 27
- 6 What Fastens Jesus to Me and What Loosens Him from Me 28
- 7 Praise to Jesus Christ 31
- 8 Jesus! the Very Thought of Thee 32
- 9 Jesus, My Shepherd, Husband, Friend 34

Chapter Two: I Have a Loving Heavenly Father 37
- 10 God Is Faithful and Good to Me 38
- 11 God's Love (1) 40
- 12 God's Love (2) 41
- 13 God's Love (3) 43
- 14 God's Love (4) 45
- 15 God's Love (5) 47

Chapter Three: God Talks to Me and I Talk to Him 51
- 16 Where God Meets Me to Talk 52
- 17 Why Do I Pray? 54
- 18 It Helps Me to Hear God's Voice 56
- 19 The Spirit of True Worship 58
- 20 Praise Is the Language of Heaven 60
- 21 God and My Searching, Restless, Praising Heart ...63
- 22 God's Kingdom, Power, and Glory 66
- 23 When I Look Up into the Heavens 68
- 24 Praise God! 71
- 25 Lord! You Are Holy 74
- 26 Bless the Lord! 77

PART TWO: IN PRAISE OF THE SPIRIT WHO FREES ME ...81

Chapter Four: The Holy Spirit Does New Things in Me and for Me ...83
27 He Saves Me! He Does—No Matter How I Feel ...84
28 Heaven Springs Up in My Heart ...87
29 How Much More! ...89
30 God's Gifts and Grace ...91
31 He Makes Me Happy and Thankful ...93

Chapter Five: The Joy of the Lord Is My Strength ...97
32 Oh! Be Joyful in the Lord ...98
33 I Am a Happy Christian! ...100
34 Let Us Love and Sing and Wonder ...102
35 Why Am I Sometimes Ungrateful? (1) ...103
36 Why Am I Sometimes Ungrateful? (2) ...106
37 Be Glad, Sing, and Dance for Joy! ...108
38 Laughter and Cheer ...111

Chapter Six: Victory! Deliverance! ...115
39 God Protects Me ...116
40 God Is with Me in My Temptations ...119
41 One Way God Develops Patience in Me ...122
42 My Foes and Fears Defeated in Christ! ...124
43 Be Happy! Someone Has Found God ...127
44 The Salvation of Our Children ...130
45 Victory over Temptation ...133
46 Great Is Thy Faithfulness ...136
47 God Gives Me Faith ...138
48 God Gives Me Everything ...141
49 I Am Made for Faith and Not for Fear ...143

Sources ...147

The little I now profess
to know about God
has the effect
of making my religion predominately
an affair
of gratitude.

> L. P. Jacks (age 92)
> in *Near the Brink*

PART ONE

*In praise of the God
who loves me*

CHAPTER ONE

Jesus Is My Friend

The God who helps those
who help themselves
is either
a monster or
a mouse.
Whatever else God is,
He is a friend
who helps him
who has no
helper.

David A. Redding

A contemporary writer of extraordinary power, David Redding has written several books and magazine articles, and preaches the gospel in up-to-date language.

1 He Is My Friend! (1)

PRAISE FROM PROPHET

Having said this,
   Martha went to call her sister
   Mary,
   saying quietly:
     "The Teacher is here;
     it is you He is calling for."

               John 11:28

PRAISE BY PEN

When Jesus is present,
   all is well,
   nothing seems difficult;
But when Jesus is not present,
   everything is hard.
When Jesus does not talk to us
by the Inner Voice,
   all other comfort is
   worthless.
All Jesus has to do is
   speak one word.
      That does it!
      What consolation!
Mary is a case in point:
   She got right up from her
   place of weeping
   as soon as she heard those lovely words,
     "The Master is here,
     He's calling for you."
Happy hour
   when Jesus calls us!
     Our tears translate into joy.

        Thomas à Kempis, *Of the Imitation of Christ*, Book
        II, Chapter VII, 1

Thomas à Kempis (1380-1471), German
mystic, received his early education from the

Brethren of the Common Life and entered
the Augustinian monastery near Zwolle,
Holland. His *De Imitatione Christi* (*Of the
Imitation of Christ*) occupies a place in the
front ranks among devotional manuals.

PRAISE THROUGH PRAYER

My God and my all!
> St. Francis of Assissi

St. Francis of Assissi (1182-1226) founded
the Franciscan order. After a frivolous youth
and a year as a military prisoner, he
experienced a deep religious awakening.
Divorcing himself from society, he nursed
lepers, begged for the poor, and restored
ruined churches. He and his companions in
1210 received the sanction of the pope to
form an order devoted to a life of apostolic
poverty and the preaching of repentance.

2 He Is My Friend! (2)

PRAISE FROM PROPHET

What is the Kingdom of Heaven like?
Well, it is like hidden treasure,
treasure hidden in a field.
A man comes along,
>   stumbles onto something.
>   Eureka! It's treasure.

>   Naturally, he covers it up
>   hurriedly so nobody else will
>   find it.
>   Then he sells everything
>   he owns, all the while

chuckling to himself with joy.
Finally, he buys the field!
Matthew 13:44

PRAISE BY PEN

There is just no comparison
between the world and Jesus.

There isn't.
To be without Jesus is
    hell;
To be with Jesus is
    heaven.
If Jesus is with you,
    no enemy can hurt you.
To find Jesus is to
    find treasure;
        In fact, the best,
        the very best,
        treasure!

Now, what about those who
    lost Jesus?
        What a loss!
        More than the
        whole world
        is
        that loss.

Without Jesus
    one is
    really
    poor;
With Jesus
    one is
    really
    rich!

Thomas à Kempis, *Of the Imitation of Christ*, Book II, Chapter VIII, 2

PRAISE THROUGH PRAYER

Heavenly King,

The One-alongside-me,
Spirit of Truth,
The One everywhere,
The One in all things,
The Best Treasure,
Choirmaster of life:
> Come and live in me,
> Wash the stains away,

> Save me.

St. John Chrysostom, *Liturgy*

St. John Chrysostom (347-407), deacon and priest at Antioch and later patriarch of Constantinople, was the most popular preacher of his age. His eloquence won for him the name "Chrysostom" (golden-mouthed) soon after his death. His writings—homilies and commentaries—are noted for their practical value for everyday life.

---

3 He Is My Friend (3)

PRAISE FROM PROPHET

> I love you
> just as
> My Father loves me.
> Live in My love.
> John 15:9

PRAISE BY PEN

Whatever you love,
love it for
Jesus' sake.
> And love Jesus
> just for Himself.

Jesus Christ alone
is your
Supreme Love;
    And He alone proves to be
    good
    and faithful;
        indeed, faithful like
        no other friend!

For Jesus and *through* Jesus
    see both your friends and your foes
    as if they were close to you.
        Why?
        Just this: so you will
        pray for them
        asking God to open their
        minds
        and hearts
        to Him.

Never desire to be
    recognized
    above the rest;
        Only God should have that
        recognition.
        There just isn't
        any other person
        in the universe
        like Him.
Nor desire that even
    one person
    single you out from
    the rest;

And you mustn't
single
out any one person from
the rest either.
    Just let Jesus live in
        you,
    And see Jesus in
        every good person.

                Thomas à Kempis, *Of the Imitation of Christ,* Book II, Chapter VIII, 4

PRAISE THROUGH PRAYER

When I try to see You, Lord,
   I see
      goodness
      grace
      love
      kindness.
   My! How You love people.

When I think of You some more,
   I see
      gentleness
      tenderness
      patience
      endurance under the most trying of circumstances;
   I also see
      mercies—so many of them!
      and compassion—a great deal of it
      and always tenderness.

Glory be to You,
   O Lord.
      Amen.

Lancelot Andrewes, *Private Prayers*

Lancelot Andrewes (1555-1626), an English bishop, was the chaplain of Queen Elizabeth and the dean of Westminster. Under James I, his name heads the list of scholars assigned to translate the Authorized Version of the Bible, his part being the books of the Old Testament as far as II Kings.

---

4 Praise for Who My Friend Is

PRAISE FROM PROPHET

The Lord is great,

and we must
Praise Him a great deal.
> I Chronicles 16:25a

PRAISE BY PEN

Jesus is a perfect picture of God.
When it comes to created things,
> He is *the* Creation,
> superior in every way.

Actually, by Jesus
God
created everything:
> in heaven,
> in earth;

things that can be seen,
things that can't:
> kings
> kingdoms
> unseen spiritual powers
> authorities—

all these things were
created
by Him and
for Him.
> Actually, He existed
> before all these things;
> and they all
> work right
> when properly related
> to Him.

He is the Head of
the Church,
> which, figuratively, we call
> "His Body."

He was the first to be
raised from the dead,
and in that way,
> He is another very important
> > "first."

Why? That in everything—

absolutely everything—He
will be seen as
    "First."
And why must He be seen as
    first?

Well, in Him was
    the full nature of God
    —God decided that.
    Through Him God made another
    decision—to bring the
    whole creation back to
    Himself—
        the creation in heaven
        the creation on earth—
    that resulted in reconciliation
    and peace which came by
    our Friend
        dying on a terrible cross!
        a cross on which Jesus
        actually gave His blood.
                Colossians 1:15-20

PRAISE THROUGH PRAYER

Oh, do give thanks to the Lord!
    He is so good.
    His love will never fail;
        nothing can outlast it. . . .
Everybody ought to thank the Lord!
    His love is steady and sure.
    His works are truly wonderful,
        and He does them for His
        children.
Amen.
                Psalm 107:1, 8

5 Christ Is with Me

PRAISE FROM PROPHET

Oh,
Lord
my
God:
> I came to You in desperate need of help,
> and You healed me!
> > Psalm 30:2

PRAISE BY PEN

Christ is with me, Christ is in me
> Christ is behind me
> Christ is ahead of me.

Christ is beside me, Christ will win me over
> Christ will comfort me
> Christ will restore me.

Christ is underneath me, Christ is over me
> Christ is with me when all is peaceful
> Christ is with me when I'm in danger.

Christ is in the hearts of all who love me
> Christ is in the words of my friends
> Christ is in the words of strangers.

I put a rope around myself and tie it to the Name
> The strong name of the trinity.
I make my pleas for help to the trinity,
> The three in one, the one in three
By whom all nature was created,
> Eternal Father, Spirit, Word.
Praise to You, Lord; You save me:
> I am saved by Christ my Lord.

> *St. Patrick's Breastplate*, ascribed to St. Patrick

> Though the life of St. Patrick is shrouded in legend and uncertainty, he was probably born in Britain during the late fourth century. At the age of sixteen he was captured by Irish pirates and sold as a slave. After about six years he escaped, but later returned to become the apostle to Ireland, planting churches throughout the country.

PRAISE THROUGH PRAYER

Lord! please help me. . . .
Lord! my God,
 I will always be thankful
 to You.
  Amen.
               Psalm 30:10b, 12b

6 What Fastens Jesus to Me and What Loosens Him from Me?

PRAISE FROM PROPHET

I am praying for you that
 out of God's storehouse of
 riches
 He will strengthen you
  with might
  through His Spirit
  on the inside of you;
 And I am also asking that
  Christ will live
  at the very center of your being
  by faith.

I am praying for more, that
 you will be rooted and
 grounded
 in love; that
you will have power to

    understand (with all God's people)
        the breadth
        the length
        the height
        the depth of God's love;
and also that
    you will know Christ's love
        which goes beyond knowledge.

Now, I am praying that you have all this
    in order that you will be
    filled right up with God Himself.
        Ephesians 3:16-19

PRAISE BY PEN

Really to exercise your will,
to have a very great desire
for Jesus
and for Jesus alone;
    then to have Him,
    actually to see Him,
        in all His beauty and loveliness,
        with your inner eye—
        well! there you have the secret,
        the secret of what fastens and ties Him
        to yourself.
The greater your desire,
the tighter Jesus is fastened;
    the less your desire,
    the looser He is tied to you.

THEREFORE, any attitude or feeling
that holds you back, and
draws you down from
    your soul's natural ascent
    towards Jesus
        (that downward pull comes
        by focusing on yourself, and
        tries to loosen and untie
        you from Jesus)—
    well! any such downward

pull can't come from God;
it comes from your
enemy.

BUT, if an attitude,
   feeling, or
   angel's revelation
      increases your desire,
      ties the knot of love or
      devotion to Jesus
      tighter;
   if it opens your
   soul's eyes
      wider
      to spiritual knowledge;
   if it makes you
   humbler—really humbler inside—
      then! you can be sure
      your desire comes
      from God.

              Walter Hilton, *The Scale of Perfection*

Walter Hilton (c. 1340-1396) lived in England and wrote on the deep things of God. *The Scale* has been called by *The Encyclopedia Britannica* the "finest treatise on contemplation during the late Middle Ages."

PRAISE THROUGH PRAYER

Jesus! the very thought of Thee
   With sweetness fills my breast,
But sweeter far Thy face to see
   And in Thy presence rest.

              St. Bernard of Clairvaux

St. Bernard of Clairvaux (1090-1153) founded and became the first abbot of the monastery of Clairvaux in 1115. He is remembered for his mystical fervor, rigid asceticism, and sterling defense of the orthodox faith. Among the hymns ascribed to him are "Jesus, the Very Thought of Thee" and "O Sacred Head, Now Wounded."

7 Praise to Jesus Christ

PRAISE FROM PROPHET

What is God's Plan?
    To make something known:
        A great and grand secret,
        at once rich and mysterious.
        He is making it known to
        everyone.
And here it is!
    Christ actually lives in you,
    and listen to what that means—
        this is
        your proof that you will
        share God's glory with Him.
                Colossians 1:27

PRAISE BY PEN

Hear the Old Testament prophets—

    They looked at the sun
    and said:
        "He is the Sun of Righteousness
        with healing in His wings."

    They looked at the stars
    and said:
        "He will be the morning star
        to tell us the exciting news that
        the new day is coming."

    They looked at the mountains
    and said:
        "He will be the great mountain in Israel
        and to Him the nations will come."

    They looked at the rock
    and said:
        "He is the rock of strength
        in a land of tired people."

They saw the bold, raging lion
and said:
> "He is the Lion
> of Judah."

They saw the lamb surrendering himself
and said:
> "He is the Lamb of God
> that takes away the sins of the world."
>> A. W. Tozer, *God's Greatest Gift to Man*

The late Dr. Tozer was one of the twentieth century's greatest preachers. A self-educated man, he possessed a grand deposit of theological and spiritual knowledge, and he shared generously from that deposit as writer, editor and preacher.

PRAISE THROUGH PRAYER

> Do let's give thanks
> to the Father of our Lord,
> Jesus Christ.
>> He has blessed us
>> in Christ
>> with every spiritual
>> and heavenly gift there is
>> in the world called
>> heaven.
>> Amen.
>>> Ephesians 1:3

8 Jesus! the Very Thought of Thee

PRAISE FROM PROPHET

I am very certain of this:
Nothing—but nothing!—can
separate me from God's love.
> Death won't do it,
> nor will the rigors of this life.

No supernatural powers can
do it.
There is no high that can rob me of His love,
and no low.
My present circumstances can't do it,
nor can my future circumstances.

Actually, there is nothing in all creation
that can separate me from God's love!
    Remember! this love I'm talking about
    is God's love
        which I see so clearly in
        Jesus Christ, my Lord.
Romans 8:38-39

PRAISE BY PEN

Jesus! the very thought of Thee
With sweetness fills my breast,
But sweeter far Thy face to see
And in Thy presence rest.

Tongue never spoke, ear never heard,
Never from heart o'erflowed,
A dearer name, a sweeter word,
Than Jesus, Son of God.

O hope of every contrite heart,
To penitents how kind;
To those who seek, how good Thou art
But what to those who find?

Ah! this no tongue can utter; this
No mortal page can show;
The love of Jesus, what it is,
None but His loved ones know.

Jesus! our only joy be Thou,
As Thou our prize will be;
Jesus! be Thou our glory now,
And through eternity.
St. Bernard of Clairvaux

PRAISE THROUGH PRAYER

It is right, and there is wholeness in
giving thanks to the Lord.
I want to sing songs of praise to
Him.
    He is my real authority.

In the morning
    I thank Him for His
    sure and steady love;

In the evening
    I thank Him for His
    faithfulness.

I thank Him to the
accompaniment of
    the lute
    the harp
        and the melody of the
    lyre.
                Psalm 92:1-3

9 Jesus, My Shepherd, Husband, Friend

PRAISE FROM PROPHET

Something great happens
inside you
when you believe with all your heart
in Jesus.

    He becomes the most important
        stone
    in your building.
               From I Peter 2:7

PRAISE BY PEN

How sweet the name of Jesus sounds

In a believer's ear!
It soothes his sorrows, heals his wounds,
And drives away his fear.

It makes the wounded spirit whole,
And calms the troubled breast;
'Tis manna to the hungry soul,
And to the weary rest.

Dear name, the rock on which I build,
My shield and hiding place;
My never-failing treasury, filled
With boundless stores of grace.

Jesus, my Shepherd, Husband, Friend,
My Prophet, Priest and King,
My Lord, my life, my way, my end,
Accept the praise I bring.

Weak is the effort of my heart,
And cold my warmest thought;
But when I see thee as Thou art,
I'll praise Thee as I ought.

Till then I would Thy love proclaim
With every fleeting breath;
And may the music of Thy name
Refresh my soul in death.

                    John Newton, *Olney Hymns*

John Newton (1725-1807) followed the sea (including a number of years as servant to a slave-trader) until 1760, when he came under the influence of George Whitefield and John Wesley. In 1764 he was ordained deacon and given the curacy of Olney, where, in collaboration with William Cowper, he wrote the *Olney Hymns*, a landmark in English hymnody.

PRAISE THROUGH PRAYER

Thank You, Lord,
for the
    multitude

of Your
tender mercies.
Amen.

J.D. Robertson, *Minister's Worship Handbook*

Dr. Robertson is a Presbyterian minister and a teacher of young people studying for the gospel ministry in America. He was born in Scotland and is an articulate preacher.

CHAPTER TWO

I Have a Loving Heavenly Father

This is assuredly
a law
in God's kingdom
that
love
produces
joy.

Mauree Johnson

Mrs. Johnson and her husband live on a farm in Georgia. Her pen reveals her intimate knowledge of God.

10 God Is Faithful and Good to Me

PRAISE FROM PROPHET

This one thing is sure:
Goodness and mercy
   are going to
   follow me
      every
      single
      day
      of
      my
      life!
                  Psalm 23:6

PRAISE BY PEN

Lord! Your mercy is in the heavens,
   Your faithfulness is as high as
   the clouds.
   Your goodness is as big as the
   great mountains.
   Your judgments come right out of the
   center of the universe.

Lord! You preserve both man
   and animals.

God! Your love and kindness are
   altogether good.
   That's why Your children
      trust You.
   That's why we feel
      comfortable
      under the shadow of Your wings.
   That's why we are
      abundantly satisfied,
      for when we sit up to the
      table
      in Your house

>   we have more than enough
>   to eat.
> That's why we experience
>   lots of
>   pleasures,
>   for You invite us to drink from
>   the river of Your pleasures.
> That's also why we have Light,
>   for You provide
>   light

Oh! keep on being loving and kind
    to all who know You,
and please continue making
    good people
    good.
Don't let me get proud—
    pride can kick me
    with a heavy foot!—
And don't let the wicked people
    remove me from Your presence—
    tie their hands!

The people who do bad things
    fall:
        they get demoted,
        they never get promoted
        again.
                Psalm 36:5-12

PRAISE THROUGH PRAYER

Oh, enter then His gates with praise,
Approach with joy His courts unto;
Praise, laud and bless His name always,
For it is seemly so to do.

For why? The Lord our God is good;

His mercy is forever sure;
His truth at all times firmly stood,
And shall from age to age endure.
W. Kethe (1561)

William Kethe is especially remembered for the lovely way he put some psalms into verse for hymn singing.

---

11 God's Love (1)

PRAISE FROM PROPHET

Be thankful to the
God and Father
of
our Lord, Jesus Christ,
   the Father who shows me mercy,
   the Father who gives me every comfort.
II Corinthians 1:3

PRAISE BY PEN

Thank You, Heavenly Father,
   Father of my Lord, Jesus Christ,
   for being so good as to remember
   me,
   because I need all the help
   I can get.

Father! You are very kind to me,
   You give me every comfort.
   Thank You.
      Even though I am unworthy,
      Your comfort
      refreshes me.
I will always thank You and
honor You;
   also Your only Son,
   and the Holy Spirit, my Comforter.

Lord, God! You are holy and
You love me;
    Whenever You enter my heart,
    I am happy from head to toe.

Lord! You are
    my honor,
    the joy of my heart,
    my hope,
    the protection I need when things go wrong.
Thomas à Kempis, Of the Imitation of Christ,
Book III, Chapter V, 1

PRAISE THROUGH PRAYER

Low before Him with our praises we fall,
Of whom, and in whom, and through whom are all;
Of whom, the Father; and through whom, the Son;
In whom, the Spirit, with these ever One.
Abelard, "Hymn for Saturday Vespers"

Peter Abelard (1079-1142), French philosopher and theologian, was a distinguished teacher who attracted large crowds to his lectures. Secretly married to Heloise, he was persecuted by her enraged uncle and eventually withdrew to a monastic life. His liberal views were denounced as heretical by Bernard of Clairvaux. As theologian Abelard is noteworthy for his doctrine of revelation and his conception of the relation between faith and knowledge.

---

12   God's Love (2)

PRAISE FROM PROPHET

My yoke wears easily,
My burden carries lightly.
Matthew 11:30

PRAISE BY PEN

Love is grand and great!
Indeed, very great, and
thoroughly good.
    It makes everything that is heavy
        light.
    It carries smoothly what otherwise would have a
        rough and bumpy ride.
    It shoulders burdens
        effortlessly.
    It makes everything that is bitter
        sweet and tasty.

Jesus' love is noble!
    It motivates one to do
        great things.
    It stirs one to something else, too—
        always to be longing
        for
        a more perfect, pure and transparent lifestyle.

Love desires largeheartedness,
    and refuses to be robbed of that lovely
        attitude
        by anything small or
        by a mean spirit.

Love wants to be free,
    free from all loves that
        prevent
        the One True Love.
    Those enemy loves
        hinder
        inward sight!
    Loving things, for example, can
        entangle us!
    A wrong love focus can
        also
        be the cause of a
        cold spirit
        when things go against us.

Nothing is
> sweeter than love,
> more courageous than love,
> higher than love,
> wider than love
> happier than love,
> richer than love;
> to sum it all up, nothing is
>> better in heaven and earth than love!

Why? Because
> love is born of God, and
> love lives in God
>> Who is in charge of
>> everything.
>>> Thomas à Kempis, *Of the Imitation of Christ*,
>>> Book III, Chapter V, 3

PRAISE THROUGH PRAYER

> Love divine! all loves excelling,
> Joy of heaven to earth come down;
> Fix in us Your humble dwelling,
> All Your faithful mercies crown.
>> Charles Wesley (1747)

Charles Wesley (1708-1788) had an experience similar to that of his brother at Aldersgate and joined with him in his great revival campaigns. The greatest contribution Charles made to the Christian church is 6,000 hymns, 4,000 of which have been published.

13 God's Love (3)

PRAISE FROM PROPHET

Have you really
realized
> how much God loves

> you?
> Well, He loves you so much that He
> calls you
> His children.
> > And that, in fact, is
> > precisely what we are.
> > > I John 3:1a

PRAISE BY PEN

Free! Unbound!
That's what the loving person is.
> He flies,
> He runs,
> He is full of joy.
More, the loving person
> Gives all and gets all,
> And what he has satisfies him fully.
Why?
> Because he rests in and
> trusts completely
> The Ruler of all things;
> > He is the One from
> > Whom all things come.
> But the loving person doesn't
> > focus
> > on the things he gets;
> Rather, he turns his
> attention
> > to the Giver.
> Often love knows
> no bounds,
> > but is fervent beyond all
> > measure.
> Love feels no
> burden,
> thinks nothing of
> trouble,
> attempts what is above its
> strength,

makes no excuses about
impossibilities.

Why is this?
    Well, love believes all things that need doing are
    right for love's sake, and
    possible for love's sake.
    Therefore,
        love is able to undertake
        anything,
        love is able to complete many
        things,
        love is able to bring many things to
        conclusion;
    but the one who does not love
        faints, and
        lies down on the job.
Thomas à Kempis, Of the Imitation of Christ, Book III Chapter V, 4

PRAISE THROUGH PRAYER

You I would be always blessing;
Serve You as Your hosts above:
Pray, and praise You, without ceasing;
Glory in Your perfect love.
Charles Wesley (1747)

14 God's Love (4)

PRAISE FROM PROPHET

Love never throws in the sponge.
To the contrary,
    love's faith is unfaltering,
    love's hope is never broken,
    love's patience never fails.
I Corinthians 13:7

PRAISE BY PEN

Love is alert,
    it never falls asleep at the
    switch,
    but it does get its rest.
Though weary,
    love is not tired;
Though pressured,
    love is not in jail with tension;
Though alarmed,
    love is not confused.
But as a lively flame
and a burning torch,
    love has the force to
    go right on up, and
    passes securely through everything.

The man who loves
    knows what his heart
    cries after.
    It is a loud cry
    in the ears of God;
        it is the ardent
        affection
    of the soul that speaks
    and says,
        "My God! the One I love
        supremely;
        You are all mine,
        I am all thine."
            Thomas à Kempis, *Of the Imitation of Christ*, Book III, Chapter V, 5

PRAISE THROUGH PRAYER

"My Lord and my God!"
        John 20:28

15 God's Love (5)

PRAISE FROM PROPHET

Love is not touchy and grumpy.
  It refuses to insist on its
  own way;
  It also refuses to be
  resentful, to feel injury or
  insult.
             I Corinthians 13:5

PRAISE BY PEN

What is love?
  It is active,
    sincere,
    affectionate,
    pleasant,
    amiable;
  It is more—it is courageous,
    patient,
    faithful,
    wise,
    willing to suffer a long time,
    manly and strong,
    never self-seeking, for
    self-seeking is
    self-defeating—
    then love vanishes.

What is love?
  It is thoughtful,
    considering all the factors;
  It is humble;
  It is strictly honorable and
    honest;
  It refuses to yield to
    softness;
  It has nothing to do with

>   inappropriate, thoughtless, and
>   unreasonable
>   humor;
>   It shuns empty, purposeless
>   trivia;
>   It is sober;
>   It is pure in taste and
>   lifestyle,
>   unpretentious and
>   simple;
>   It permits the five senses
>   to respond only to the good,
>   the true,
>   the beautiful.
> What is love?
>   It is submissive,
>   obedient to its
>   superiors;
>   It sees itself as
>   no better than
>   others;
>   It is devout and
>   thankful
>   to God,
>   always trusting and
>   hoping in Him,
>   even when what He gives
>   is without chocolate coating.
>   Come to think about it,
>   love couldn't really function
>   if there were nothing
>   sour
>   to
>   sweeten.
>
> > Thomas à Kempis, *Of the Imitation of Christ*, Book III, Chapter V, 7

PRAISE THROUGH PRAYER

Loving Savior, You did give,
Your own life that we might live,

And Your hands outstretched to bless
Bear the cruel nails' impress.
                    Jane E. Leeson

Jane Leeson (1807-1882) was a hymnwriter who also translated many hymns from the Latin.

CHAPTER THREE

God Talks to Me, and I Talk to Him

I believe truly that
Satan
cannot endure it [song],
and so slips out of the room—
more or less!—
where there is true song. . . .

Prayer rises more easily,
more spontaneously,
after one has
let those wings,
words and music,
carry one out of oneself
into that upper air.

Amy Carmichael

Amy Carmichael (1867-1951) was a missionary of the Church of England to India for fifty-five years. Her special achievements include rescuing girls from a life of shame in Hindu temples and establishing a home for children at Dohnavur.

16 Where God Meets Me to Talk

PRAISE FROM PROPHET

When you talk to God,
    go to your room
    close the door,
    pray to your Father
        quietly and privately.
He sees you there;
    others don't need to
    see you.
In fact, He Himself will
    reward you;
you don't need to try to
    get your own reward by being
    seen.
                Matthew 6:6

PRAISE BY PEN

Lord, especially gladden the
hearts
and support those in their
    prayer rooms
        working for You on their knees.
    In those prayer rooms
        Your truth and
        grace
        are made known to them.
    There, they are
        daily
        anointed with fresh
        oil.
    There, they are
        strengthened and
        renewed.
    They receive
        answers to prayer and help

      by believing You.
    And blessings You give
    they use, in turn, to
        bless
        their friends and neighbors,
        or anyone at all.

Lord! draw us all
    to our own prayer rooms
    where You and Your
    Father
    come very near us.

                Andrew Murray, *With Christ in the School of Prayer*

PRAISE THROUGH PRAYER

Thank you, Savior!
    I thank You with my
    whole heart,
        for keeping Your
        appointment
        with me in the
        Inner Room.
    That place is my
        school room
        where You come and
        teach me by myself.
    You also make
    God
    known to me
    there.
        Amen.

                Andrew Murray, With Christ in the School of Prayer

---

Andrew Murray (1828-1917), Dutch Reformed minister in South Africa, was noted for his itinerant evangelism throughout his country, his deep interest in the social and educational betterment of his people, and his many devotional books which emphasize the deepening of the spiritual life.

17 Why Do I Pray?

PRAISE FROM PROPHET

Whatever you ask,
ask it in My Name,
   so that My Father
   will be honored
   through Me.
                John 14:13

PRAISE BY PEN

A life aimed at
   God's honor only
   cannot be achieved
   by any effort of our own.
       Jesus Christ can give us
       that life.
Yes! in Him it can be
   found.
       Actually, His life is
       our life.
Praise God!
       He gave *Himself* for us;
       He Himself is now our life.

Let's go deeper:
   The discovery of my selfishness,
   The confession of my selfishness,
   The denial of my selfishness
   —all this because I would
      otherwise
      make myself God;
      I am self-seeking and
      self-trusting—
well! all that must go;
yet, I haven't got what it
   takes

        to make it go.
It is His incoming and
    indwelling,
It is His Presence,
It is His Rule in my heart,
It is the Lord Jesus,
    who honored His Father
    on earth,
        and Who now is honored
        alongside the Father,
        so that He can honor Him
        in us.
Well, this is Jesus Himself
    coming in,
        isn't it?
He can take out of us
    all self-honoring tendencies;
He can give us, instead,
    His own God-honoring life and
        Spirit.

Summed up, here is the whole point:
    Jesus longs to honor God the Father.
    He does that by hearing our
        prayers.
    Jesus will also teach us to
        live
        and to pray to honor God.
              Andrew Murray, *With Christ in the School of Prayer*

PRAISE THROUGH PRAYER

Help me, Lord!
    You are the honored God,
        the Father of honor,
        my God and my Father.
    Accept the desire of Your
    child
    who now sees that
    Your honor is indeed
        the only thing worth living for.
        I want that great truth to

      overshadow me.
      I want that great truth to
      fill the temple of my
      heart.
      I want to live in that great truth
      as it was made clear in
      Christ.
Help me, Lord!
      I want You Yourself to bring to
      flower
      in me exactly what You desire
      most,
          so that I will find Christ's
          honor
          by seeking the honor of His
          Father.
          Amen.

                Andrew Murray, *With Christ in the School of Prayer*

18   It Helps Me to Hear God's Voice

PRAISE FROM PROPHET

Happiness is yours because
    your eyes see,
    your ears hear.
Listen! Many prophets,
    many of God's good people,
    wanted very much to
        see what you see, and
        hear what you hear,
    but they neither
        saw
        nor
        heard.

            Matthew 13:16-17

PRAISE BY PEN

I will listen to what the
Lord God
says by the Inner Voice.

Happy is the one
   who hears
   the Lord speaking
   by the Inner Voice.

Happy is the one
   who receives from
   God's lips
   kind words that console.

Happy are the ears
   that gladly receive
   the pulses of the
   divine whisper,
      and give no heed to the
      whisperings of this
      world.

Happy—very happy!—are the ears
   which listen
   not to the Outside Voice
      but to the Inside Voice
      teaching truth within.

Happy are the eyes
   which are shut to
   the Outside World
      but open wide to the Inside World.

Happy are those who go
very far into the
Inward World,
   and work at preparing themselves
      more and more
      by daily exercises
      for receiving heavenly secrets.

Happy are those who are
>   glad
>   to have time to spare for
>   God,
> and who shake off all wordly
>   hindrances.

>> Thomas à Kempis, *Of the Imitation of Christ,* Book III, Chapter II, 1

PRAISE THROUGH PRAYER

Lord, my God!
>   You are to me
>   all that is
>   good.

>> Thomas à Kempis, *Of the Imitation of Christ,* Book III, Chapter III, 5

19 The Spirit of True Worship

PRAISE FROM PROPHET

Jacob woke from his sleep
>   and said,
>>   "Without a doubt the Lord is
>>   right here!
>>   But I didn't know it."
. . . Again he spoke:
>   "This—this very place!—is
>   none other than the
>   house of God,
>>   and also the gate swinging wide open to
>>   heaven."

>> Genesis 28:16-17

PRAISE BY PEN

Worship is . . .
>the quickening of conscience by God's holiness;
>the nourishment of mind with His truth;
>the purifying of imagination by His beauty;
>the opening of the heart to His love;
>the surrender of the will to His purpose;

and all of this gathered up in adoration—
the most selfless emotion of which our nature is capable,
and therefore the chief
>remedy
>>for the self-centeredness
>>which is our original sin
>>and the source of all actual sin.

>>>>Archbishop William Temple, *Readings in St. John's Gospel.*

William Temple (1881-1944), Archbishop of Canterbury, helped organize the World Council of Churches, endeavored to make the Church of England a growing force in the nation's life, and lent his support to many social reforms.

PRAISE THROUGH PRAYER

God! Author of eternal light,
>lead me in worship today
>so that
>>my lips will praise You,
>>my life will please You,
>>my meditations will honor You.

This I ask through
Christ my Lord.
   Amen.

Sarum Breviary (Eleventh century).

Sarum is an old ecclesiastical name for
Salisbury, England. A *breviary* is a prayer
book prepared for daily use.

---

20   Praise Is the Language of Heaven

PRAISE FROM PROPHET

The streams all run into the sea,
but the sea never gets full;
Always the streams flow to their place,
they go back again and again and again.
                    Ecclesiastes 1:7

PRAISE BY PEN

The Lord gives many beautiful things to the
    Church;
    They cannot get buried in oblivion;
    indeed, He asks us to
    thank
    Him for them!
The beams from big lights
    are like pipes or channels
    through which the light flows
    to others.

Well, thanksgiving is the
    beam
    of an enlightened person.
Thanksgiving is poured through the
    channel.
        That's only natural:
        God uses *His* channel
        to pour out His mercies
        on us,

Now we use our channel
to thank Him back.
Everything naturally returns
to its original source, just as
Ecclesiastes says:
> "The streams all run into the sea,
> but the sea never gets full;
> Always the streams flow to their place,
> they go back again and again and again."

A straight line,
    drawn on and on,
        gets weaker and weaker.
Not so a circle:
    returning to its beginning
        point
    it recaptures its strength
        entirely.
And so it is with us.
    The further we go from God
    the weaker we get,
    until! Ah, until
    we return back to Him
        again.

Well! the best way of returning to Him
    is praising Him,
        because praise is the
        language of heaven,
        where men are perfectly at
        home
        with God.
            Edward Reynolds, *Works,* volume V

Edward Reynolds (1599-1676) was a bishop of the Church of England.

PRAISE THROUGH PRAYER

Almighty God,
    Father of every mercy,
    we are undeserving servants,
        but we give You humble and
        heartfelt thanks

for all Your goodness and
love and
kindness
to us and to all people.
We thank you from our hearts for
creating us,
preserving us,
and for all the ways You make us
happy in this life.
But above all,
we are grateful for Your
love,
too great even to be
estimated,
which expressed itself in
redeeming
the world by our
Lord, Jesus Christ.

Thank you, too, for the
channels
through which You pour Your
grace.
Also, thank You for the hope of
heaven
with its rewards and honors.

Lord, we ask with all our hearts to
give us real awareness of
all Your mercies,
so that our hearts may be
genuinely thankful.
And that we can be
examples of thankfulness
not only by what we say
but by the way we live:
by giving ourselves to Your
service,
by walking before You
in holiness and goodness
every day of our lives.
All this we pray
through Jesus Christ our

Lord,
> whom, along with the Holy Spirit,
> we recognize as having
> all honor and respect
> in Your world that never ends.
Amen.
Edward Reynolds from *The Book of Common Prayer*

Bishop Reynolds wrote this prayer for the 1661 edition of *Common Prayer*.

---

21 God and My Searching, Restless, Praising Heart

PRAISE FROM PROPHET

By my very lifestyle
> I will be thankful to
> the Lord.
The thankfulness He puts in
> my heart
>> I will express with
>> my lips.
Psalm 34:1

PRAISE BY PEN

You are great, Lord;
> that is why You must be
> thanked greatly.
Your power is great,
Your wisdom is beyond understanding.
> We want to praise You,
> we who are a part of Your
>> creation,
> we who are only men
>> and must die,
> we who must die because of
>> sin,
> we who know very well that

> You resist the proud.

Yet, we want to praise You,
> we who are a part of Your
>> creation.

It is You, Lord, who
> awakens
>> in us the
> delight of praising You,
>> because You have made us for
>> Yourself,
> and our hearts are
> restless
>> till they find rest in
>> You.

Help me, then, Lord,
> to know and understand
>> whether
> first to call to You
> or to praise You,
>> whether
> first to know You
> or to call to You.
>> But who can call to You
>> and not know You?
>> Because if I don't know
>> You,
>>> the God I picture in my
>>> mind
>>> may not be You.

On second thought,
> do we call to You
> in order to find out who You
> are?

What is clear is this:
> I couldn't call to You
> if I didn't believe in You.
> And I couldn't believe in
>> You
>>> if a preacher hadn't told me
>>> about You.

I cannot seek the Lord
and avoid praising Him,
> for those who seek
>> find,
> and finding Him
> naturally results in
> praising Him.
So, Lord, I will seek You
> and call to You;
I will call to You
> with a believing heart,
>> because preachers have
>> told me about You.
My faith, Lord,
> motivates
>> me to call to You;
You gave me that
> faith!
>> You inspire me with that
>> faith.
The way You gave me
> faith
>> was through a picture of
>> Your Son
>> in whom You lived,
>> and through the
>> ministry
>> of Your chosen preacher.
>>> St. Augustine, *Confessions,* Book 1, Chapter I

PRAISE THROUGH PRAYER

It is You, Lord, who
awakens
in us the
delight of praising You,
> because You have made us for
> Yourself,
> and our hearts are
> restless

till they find rest in
You.
    Amen.
                St. Augustine

22 God's Kingdom, Power, and Glory

PRAISE FROM PROPHET

Lord, we don't want to be
tempted;
we do want deliverance from
the evil
that could cause temptation.
    We believe You can
    deliver
    us, because You are
        in charge of the real kingdom,
        in possession of all power,
        and You are honored for the
        God You are.
                Matthew 6:13

PRAISE BY PEN

David praised the Lord
in the presence of
all the people.
David said:
    "I want to praise You, Lord,
    the God of our big family, Israel.
    I want to praise You
    for ever and ever.
    You are greatness itself, Lord;
        therefore, You have power and
        honor.
        You have victory and
        majesty.
        For everything in the heavens

>and in the earth
>belongs to You.
>Yes! the Kingdom is Yours, Lord,
>and You are the Supreme Head
>over all things.
>
>In Your hand, Lord, are
>power and might.
>>In Your hand, too, is the power
>>to make men great
>>and to give energy to
>>all.
>
>And now, Lord, we all want to thank You,
>You who are our God,
>and praise Your glorious name."
>
>>I Chronicles 29:10-13

PRAISE THROUGH PRAYER

You are the highest authority, Lord,
All honor belongs to You,
> Creator,
> Lord of heaven and earth,
> Preserver of everything,
> Father of all mercies,
>> the Father who loved
>> Your children
>> so much You sent Your
>> only Son
>> into our world
>> to make good come out of
>> sin and misery,
>> and to make possible
>> everlasting life
>> for us.

Accept, gracious God, our
> praises
> and thanksgiving for

so many kindnesses we can't
number them,
and teach us, Lord, to
love
You more and serve You
better.

All this is prayed through Jesus Christ,
our Lord.
Amen.

Archbishop John Hamilton

John Hamilton (c. 1511-1571) a contemporary of John Knox the reformer, was head of the Church in Scotland.

---

23 When I Look Up into the Heavens

PRAISE FROM PROPHET

Look! it's the glory of God.
It came from the east.
It is the glory of the God of
Israel.
Listen! you can hear Him coming:
It's like the sound of water,
like a great deal of water
ebbing and flowing.
Look once more!
The earth shines
with the glory of God.

Ezekiel 43:2

PRAISE BY PEN

Look! The heavens!
They say "God!"
They say more:
"God is glorious!"
And the stars and clouds:

They say, "God is Creator!"
This message pours out
    day after day,
    night after night.
Some knowledge!
    No, the message doesn't come by
    speech,
    nor by words,
    nor by a voice that can be heard.
        Yet! there *is* a voice
        heard over the whole earth;
        there *are* words
        heard to the ends of the world.

Look again at the heavens!
    There you see a tent
    for the sun.
        It comes out of the tent
        like a young groom
        coming out of the
        bedroom,
        like a strong man
        running at a track meet
        and winning!
        The sun rises at one
        end of the heavens,
        follows the curve of the sky to
            9 A.M.
            12 Noon
            3 P.M.
            6 P.M.
        and sets at the other end
        of the heavens.
        Is it any wonder
        nothing escapes its
        warmth?
Look once more! this time at
God's Law.
    His Law is perfect;
        refreshment comes by
        obeying it.
    God's Law is a sure
        thing;

  it makes even simple people
   wise.
 His Law is absolutely
   right;
   a happy heart comes by
   keeping it.
 God's Law is clean;
   it lasts for ever.
 God's Law is true;
   clearly, it is good.
 His Law is the ultimate;
 it is better than gold,
   even lots of it;
 it is sweeter than honey,
   even the honeycomb drippings.
 God's Law warns us;
   keep it! what great
   reward!

But, Lord, I don't always
 know
 when I break Your Law.
   Keep me from hidden
   sins.
   Keep me also from
   outright sin.
   I don't want outright sins to have
   power over me!
If You keep me from both
conscious and unconscious
sins,
   then I will be both blameless
   and innocent of any great wrong.

I want the words that come from my
 mouth,
And the meditations that come from my
 heart,
   to be 100% acceptable to You,
   Lord, my Rock and my Redeemer.

     Psalm 19

PRAISE THROUGH PRAYER

Yes, Lord! Yes, indeed!
   Blessing
      glory
   wisdom
      thanksgiving
   honor
      power
   might
all are characteristics of
   You,
and will be for ever and ever.
   Yes, Lord!
      Yes, indeed!
                Revelation 7:12

24 Praise God!

PRAISE FROM PROPHET

With all my heart
I say,
   "Praise the Lord!
   Lord, my God, You are
   very great.
   You are dressed in
   honor and majesty."
               Psalm 104:1

PRAISE BY PEN

God! we praise You.
   We acknowledge You as
   Lord, as supreme.
Father! You are eternal.
   All earth worships You.
   All angels worship You.
   All powers of the heavenly world

worship You.
All cherubim and seraphim
    continually worship You.

Lord God Almighty! To You we say
    "Holy! Holy! Holy!"
All heaven and all earth
    are full of Your majesty,
        Your glory.
That great company of people
    called apostles
        Praises You,
that grand and good fellowship of
    people called
        prophets
        Praises You.
The noble army of
    martyrs
        Praises You.

This is the way the Church,
holy as it is, and worldwide,
acknowledges You:
    As Father, majestic beyond
        calculation;
    As Father of Your only
        Son,
            who is to be adored,
            who is true;
    Also as Holy Spirit,
        our Comforting One.

Christ! You are King of
honor.
    You are the everlasting
        Son of the Father.
    When You went about the
        business
    of rescuing Your
        children,
    You humbled Yourself to be
        born
            of a young girl in
            very ordinary circumstances.

When You overcame death—
    that sharp and nasty business!—
You opened up heaven,
    with all its Kingdom blessings,
    to everyone who believes in
You!
You sit at the right hand of
    God the Father.
    His bright light of
    glory
    shines on You there.
Someday You will be
    our Judge.
    That's why we ask You
    to help us.

You rescued us by
    dying for us!
Lord! we want to be numbered
    with Your saints
        to live for eternity
        and to share Your glory and honor.
Lord! save Your people,
    bless Your heritage.
        Govern us.
        Keep our minds on You!
Day by day we praise You
    enthusiastically.
        Your Name will always
        call us to worship,
        even in the next world which won't
        end!
Lord! Keep us safe from sin
    today.
Lord! Be kind to me, very
    kind.
Lord! Even as You are kind to
    me,
        so I am putting my trust in
        You.

Lord! I have trusted in You;
    don't permit me to be

confused
now or ever.
>
> *Te Deum laudamus*

Te Deum laudamus is Latin for "You, God! We Praise." The words of this prayer are timeless. A ninth century legend—apparently it is only legend—says that St. Ambrose and St. Augustine wrote it.

PRAISE THROUGH PRAYER

Praise God, from whom all blessings flow,
Praise Him, all creatures here below,
Praise Him above, ye heavenly host,
Praise Father, Son, and Holy Ghost.
>
> Thomas Ken (c. 1674)

Thomas Ken (1637-1711), bishop of Bath and Wells, was a fearless preacher as well as an accomplished linguist and musician. It is as a hymn writer that he is best known. His hymns include "Awake, My Soul" and the familiar doxology, "Praise God from Whom All Blessings Flow."

---

25 Lord! You Are Holy

PRAISE FROM PROPHET

Holy! Holy! Holy!

That's what our Lord is,
>   our Lord who is Lord over all in
>   heaven too.

>   The whole earth is
>   full
>   of the Lord's honor and
>   glory.
>
>   Isaiah 6:3b

PRAISE BY PEN

Lord! You are holy;
>You are the one and only
>>God;
>Your acts are
>>something to behold!

Lord! You are strong,
>You are great,
>You are the highest authority,
>You are almighty!
>You are holy, Father,
>You are King of heaven and earth!

Lord! You are Three and One,
>You are all good, God.
>Yes, You are good,
>>totally good,
>>supremely good,
>You are the Lord, God,
>>alive and authentic.

Lord! You are love itself,
>You are wisdom itself,
>You are humility itself,
>You are patience itself,
>You are serenity itself,
>You are peace itself,
>You are joy and gladness themselves,
>You are fairness and moderation themselves,
>You are the source of all our abundance,
>You Yourself satisfy us.

Lord! You show us beauty,
>You show us gentleness,
>You show us protection,
>You show us help by
>guarding and defending us.
>You show us courage;
>You are heaven itself, and
>You are our hope.

Lord! You are faith to us,
    You are comfort to us,
    You are the Source of eternal life,
    You are great and wonderful, our Lord!
    What more can we say? You are
    God Almighty,
    and You are our merciful Savior.

PRAISE THROUGH PRAYER

God, I want to thank You,
You who are my Superior, and
The Lord, Jesus Christ.
    I want to thank You for
    all the benefits and kindnesses
    You give me,
    for all the pains and insults
    You have borne for me.
    You are a most kind Friend,
    You are my Brother;
    You are the one who turns
        bad things into good
        things.

Help me to know You
    more clearly,
Help me to love you
    more dearly,
Help me to follow You
    more nearly.
        Amen.

St. Richard of Chichester

St. Richard (c. 1197-1253) was an Oxford University chancellor who also served at Canterbury and later was made Bishop of Chichester.

26 Bless the Lord!

PRAISE FROM PROPHET

Bless the Lord!
    My soul cries out,
    "Bless the Lord!"
    All that is inside
    me
    cries out,
        "Bless His holy Name!"
                Psalm 103:1

PRAISE BY PEN

Bless the Lord!
    My soul cries out,
    "Bless the Lord!"
    All that is inside
        me
    cries out,
        "Bless His Holy Name!"
My soul dictates that I
    bless the Lord.
How could I forget
    all
        His benefits?
How could I forget
        the way He forgives
    all
        my sins?
How could I forget
        the way He heals
    all
        my diseases?
No! I cannot forget.
    He rescues me from
        destruction;
    He puts a crown on my

       head made of love and mercy that
       won't die;
    He satisfies me with good things
       as long as I live
       so that my youth is renewed
       and I keep as strong as an
       eagle.

The Lord sees to it that the
    overwhelmed
       are vindicated and that they are
       treated right.
God showed Moses how He
    does things;
God showed the people of Israel
    how He acts.
The Lord is kind and gracious,
    slow to get angry, and
    abounds in love that won't quit.
It's not in His nature to
    scold us all that much,
    nor to keep on being
       angry.
Actually, His punishment isn't
    equal
       to our sins,
nor does he "pay us
    back"
    for our sins.

Compare the height of the heavens
    with the greatness of His enduring
    love:
That's how big His love is for those who
follow Him.
Here's another comparison:
       east and west are as far
       removed
    as he removes your
    sin
    from you!

Yet another comparison:
    as a father has deep and

heartfelt
concern for his children,
so God has deep and
heartfelt
concern for those who obey
Him.
>You see, He knows who we are;
>He has not forgotten we are dust.
>>Psalm 103:1-14

PRAISE THROUGH PRAYER

Bless the Lord!
>My soul cries out,
>"Bless the Lord!"
>Lord! You are
>>my
>
>God, and
>You are very
>Great!
>>Amen.
>>Psalm 104:1a

PART TWO

In praise of the Spirit who frees me

CHAPTER FOUR

The Holy Spirit Does New Things in Me and for Me

"Do you expect
to go to heaven?"
someone asked a
devout Scotsman.
The reply he received
was wholly unexpected:
"Why, man,
I live there!"

                      Mauree Johnson

27 He Saves Me! He Does—No Matter How I Feel!

PRAISE FROM PROPHET

Faithful?
    The Lord is faithful
    to every word He
        speaks. . . .
Gracious?
    The Lord is gracious
    in every one of His
        actions.
                Psalm 145:13b

PRAISE BY PEN

In the evening,
I went very
unwillingly
to a small group
meeting
in Aldersgate Street.
    There one of our
    number
    was reading from Luther's
    commentary on Romans
        —actually, it was
        the preface from which
        he read.
        About fifteen minutes
        to nine,
        the fellow reading up
        front
        had come to the place where
        Luther
        describes the change
        God
        brings about in the
        heart

> through faith in
> Christ.

At that precise moment (!)
I knew in my
heart
I did in fact
trust Christ,
Christ alone for my
salvation.
> And just then too (!)
> God gave me
> assurance
> that He had taken away
> *my* sin,
>> Yes! *my* sin,
>> and saved *me*
>> from the stubborn grip
>> of sin and death.

I began to pray
with all my
might
for those who had
given me an especially
bad time.
> Next, I stood up
> and testified quite
> openly
> to everyone in our
> small group;
> I told them exactly
> how I felt
> at fifteen minutes to
> nine.

Soon the enemy of my
> soul
>> whispered, "Really, now!
>> You can't honestly believe
>> you have faith; where is your
>> joy?"

Then it was I learned an

important lesson:
> while peace and victory
> over sin
> relate to faith in the
> Captain of my salvation,
> great joy—which usually
> accompanies the first
> burst of religious experience,
> especially in those who have
> had a rough time—
>> that great joy God
>> sometimes
>> gives, and sometimes He
>> does not.
>
> Whether He does or
> doesn't
> is completely up to
> Him.

John Wesley, *Journal for May 24, 1738*

John Wesley (1703-1791), the founder of Methodism, had been disenchanted with his spiritual life. On May 24, 1738, at a Moravian meeting on Aldersgate Street in London, he underwent an intense religious experience. From that day on, through a series of preaching tours, prolific writings, and by organizational ability he spearheaded a great religious revival and the development of the Methodist movement.

PRAISE THROUGH PRAYER

Lord! Your creation—
> all of it—
gives thanks to You.
Lord! Your saints—
> all of them—
give thanks to You.
> They really tell what a
>> glorious

      Kingdom You have.
      They also tell about
         Your power.

When these things are
   told
     people begin to "see"—
        they begin to see what
        You really do.

When these things are
   told
     people begin to "see"—
        they begin to see the
        glorious splendor
        of Your Kingdom.
                Psalm 145:10-12

28 Heaven Springs Up in My Heart

PRAISE FROM PROPHET

Now then! since we are part
of such a warm, supporting
fellowship of lots of people,
    we are at perfect ease to
       lay aside
       all security crutches—

    those sins that stick
       like
       flies to fly paper—
and our wills are free
to make a real and
solid decision:

       to run, without once
       looking back, the race of
       life
       until our very last day
       when we hit the tape.
              Hebrews 12:1

PRAISE BY PEN

Our experience clearly
confirms
what the Bible teaches.
And it's the experience
not just of one or two,
but of lots and lots of
people.
    People not just of our
    time,
    but of all ages.
        People not only
        living
        but dying too.
More, *your* experience,
and *my* experience
confirm it.

And just what is confirmed?
This: The Inner Voice
tells me I belong to God,
that I am His child.
    Then, how can I help but call
    Him "Father"?
        Come to think of it,
        I called Him "Father"
        quite naturally and
        spontaneously—
I didn't wait until
I saw changes in my
life.

Well, from that Inner Assurance
that God is my Father, and I
His child—
    from that flowed
        love
        joy
        peace
        all fruit of the Spirit.
First, I heard
    "Your sins are forgiven!"

Accept You I did!
   I listen'd, and heaven sprang up in my heart.
              John Wesley, *The Witness of the Spirit,* Discourse II

PRAISE THROUGH PRAYER

Father! When we call You
"Father"
naturally and spontaneously,
   that is Your Spirit
   Himself
   telling us down deep
   inside
   that we are Your
   children.
      Amen.
              Romans 8:15b-16

29 How Much More!

PRAISE FROM PROPHET

   We are sinful,
   yet! we know how to give gifts to
   our children.
   How much more
   will our Heavenly Father give the
   Holy Spirit
   to us if we ask Him!
              Luke 11:13

PRAISE BY PEN

Just as the branch,
   already filled with sap
   from the vine,
   cries for both continued
   and increasing

> flow of sap
> so that its fruit will
> come to lovely
> ripeness,
>> so the believer,
>> happy in the possession of the
>> Spirit,
>> continuously thirsts and
>> cries for more.

Jesus our Teacher
wants
us to learn that God will
give
us exactly what He
promised—
indeed, what He
commanded!
That—no less!—must be
the measure
of our expectation and of
our prayer.
> We must be filled to
> overflowing.
> He wants us to ask this
> with the full knowledge
> that the wonderful
> HOW MUCH MORE
> flows right out
> of the Father's heart of love
> and is, in fact, His pledge
> that when we ask,
>> we most certainly receive!

Andrew Murray, *With Christ in the School of Prayer*

PRAISE THROUGH PRAYER

Lord! Just now, while I
pray,
I do indeed say in faith,
> "I have what I ask;
> the fullness of the Spirit

is mine!"
I have freedom to pray this
way
because if there is one thing
on earth
I can be sure of,
it is this:
> My Father wants me to be
> filled
> with His Spirit.
> In fact, He delights
> to give me
> His Spirit!
>> Amen.

Andrew Murray, *With Christ in the School of Prayer*

30 God's Gifts and Grace

PRAISE FROM PROPHET

> Oh! the deep riches of God.
> Oh! the deep wisdom of God.
> Oh! the deep knowledge of God.
>> Romans 11:33a

PRAISE BY PEN

Be thankful for the smallest gift;
> this is the best way to be ready
> for greater
>> gifts.

Be thankful for the smallest gift
> as if it were the biggest;
> Accept the most contemptible
>> gift
> as if it were very special.

Consider the worth of the Giver:
> Then! no gift will seem

little
or
mean.
How can a gift be little
when it comes from the
Most High God?

Even if He should give punishment,
beatings (!),
    it ought to be a matter of
        thankfulness,
because always He does only
what promotes our
        welfare,
and He permits only what is
ultimately good
for us.

Do you desire to keep God's
grace?
        Be thankful for the
        grace
        given. . . .

            Thomas à Kempis, *Of the Imitation of Christ,* Book III, Chapter III, 5

PRAISE THROUGH PRAYER

Don't forget to be merciful to me,
Lord.

Fill my heart with Your
grace.

It is not Your will that Your works
should be either
    void
    or
    vain.
        Amen.

            Thomas à Kempis, *Of the Imitation of Christ,* Book II, Chapter X, 5

31 He Makes Me Happy and Thankful

PRAISE FROM PROPHET

Lord! My God:
   I will give thanks
   to You
   forever.
                   Psalm 30:12b

PRAISE BY PEN

One kind of prayer is
thanking.
Just what is thanking?
   It is a true inward
   knowing,
   with great reverence
   and also a kind of
   lovely awe,
      an awe that turns our
      focus
      with all our might
      to do what our good Lord
      stirs
      us to do—enjoy and
      be grateful to
      Him
      with the whole of our
      inner man.
Sometimes our hearts overflow
with thanks.
   Then we must just say
   thank you out loud,
   using words like these:
      "Good Lord, I thank You!
      I want to praise You!"
Sometimes we get pretty dry
and just don't have much feeling,
   And sometimes we are tempted

by the enemy.
    At such times both reason
    and grace dictate that we
    cry to God, even
    out loud,
    rehearsing His
    beautiful
    self-giving
    death on the cross,
    also His great
    goodness.

Then! oh, then it happens:
the spoken words of thanksgiving
get right into our souls,
and we find our hearts
    quickened,
    and God's grace going to
    work,
        and we discover ourselves
        praying in the
        joy that is heaven.

Truly to enjoy our Lord
    like that
is, in His sight, to be
    thanking Him
with the joy of heaven in
    our hearts.

                Juliana of Norwich, *Revelations of Divine Love*,
                Fourteenth Revelation

Juliana of Norwich (c. 1342-1443), English mystic, was an anchoress outside the walls of St. Julian's Church in Norwich. In 1373 she claimed to have sixteen revelations in two days. Twenty years later she wrote *The Sixteen Revelations of Divine Love*.

PRAISE THROUGH PRAYER

Lord, You have given
so much

to me;
Give one more thing:
   a grateful heart.
      Amen.

George Herbert, "Gratefulness"

George Herbert (1593-1633) was a courtier to James I, but after the king's death gave himself completely to a religious life. He was appointed rector of Bemerton. His devotional poems have become religious classics and have established him, along with John Keble, as the poet of Anglican theology.

CHAPTER FIVE

The Joy of the Lord Is My Strength

It must never be forgotten
that joy
is one of the commonest
New Testament words.

William Barclay

Dr. Barclay's commentaries on the New Testament have made him famous the world over. He is also known for many other popular books and his television series, originating from his native Scotland.

---

32 Oh! Be Joyful in the Lord

PRAISE FROM PROPHET

In my imagination
I paint
a big picture of God;
My spirit gets very
happy and excited
about God who is my
Savior.
                    Luke 1:46b-47

PRAISE BY PEN

Everybody in every land
listen!
    "Let your expressions of
    praise to the Lord
    be full of joy.
    Let your expressions of
    service to the Lord
    be full of gladness.
    Let your expressions of
    praise to the Lord
    in His presence
    be full of song."

Here is more:
    "Know this—the Lord is
    God!
    Know this too—the
    Lord
    made us, we are His!
        we are His people,
        like sheep in His
        pasture."

Still more:
    "When you go to

church
enter with thanksgiving
on your lips and
a spirit of praise
in your hearts."

Why all this praise and
thanksgiving?
    Because the Lord is good,
His unwavering love will
last for ever,
His faithfulness will go
on and on, from generation to
generation.
Psalm 100

PRAISE THROUGH PRAYER

To Him who has
all that it takes
    to keep you from falling, and
    to present you quite sinless and
    spotless
    before God in all His
    glory
    with joy on your
    lips and in your heart—

to this God,
who is our Savior
through Jesus Christ our Lord,
be honor
    majesty
all control
    authority

before time began
    right now and
        in the whole of the future.

    Amen.
Jude 24-25

33 I Am a Happy Christian!

PRAISE FROM PROPHET

If I go on living,
   I live for the Lord;
If I do not go on living;
   I die for the Lord.
So this is clear:
   whether I live,
   whether I die,
      I am the Lord's.
               Romans 14:8

PRAISE BY PEN

As a Christian
I am happy in a
special kind of way,
   inexpressibly happy.
Happy in what?
   In these clear and
   complete convictions:
   The God who is
      all-powerful
      all-wise
      all-gracious
      Governor over all
      loves me!
   This God who is the lover of my
      soul
      is *always with me,*
      is never absent—
      no! not for a moment.
Well! is it any wonder I
love Him too?
   There is no one in heaven
   but God.
   There is no one on earth

I desire
but God!

Something else:
    He has made me
    like Himself;
    He has stamped
    His image
    on my heart.

Now then:
    I live for Him;
    I do only His will;
    I honor Him with
        my body and
        my spirit.
    Before long, I will
    die and go to
    Him,
    I will die in the arms of
    God.

Then!
    Good-bye to sin,
    Good-bye to pain.
Then!
    there is only one thing
    left—
    to live with Him for ever!

        John Wesley, *A Plain Account of Genuine Christianity*

PRAISE THROUGH PRAYER

"Yes, Lord!
You know I love
You!"
        John 21:16b

34 Let Us Love and Sing and Wonder

PRAISE FROM PROPHET

To Him
   who loves us,
   who has freed us
      from the prison of our sins
      by dying on the cross;
To Him
   who made a kingdom for us,
   and put us in it as priests
      to serve the God and Father of Jesus;
To Him
   must go glory and control of all things
   for ever and for ever.
      Amen.
                   Revelation 1:5b-6

PRAISE BY PEN

Let us love and sing and wonder;
Let us praise the Savior's name!
He has hushed the law's loud thunder,
He has quenched Mount Sinai's flame:
He has washed us with His blood,
He has brought us nigh to God.

Let us love the Lord who bought us,
Dying for our rebel race;
Called us by His word and taught us
By the Spirit of His grace,
He has washed us with His blood,
He presents our souls to God.

Let us sing, though fierce temptation
Threaten hard to bear us down;
For the Lord, our strong Salvation,
Holds in view the Conqueror's crown.
He who washed us with His blood
Soon will bring us home to God.

Let us praise, and join the chorus
Of the saints enthroned on high:
Here they trusted Him before us;
Now their praises fill the sky:—
"Thou hast washed us with Thy blood!
Thou art worthy, Lamb of God."
>>
John Newton, *Olney Hymns* (1779)

PRAISE THROUGH PRAYER

Lord, praise comes up in my
heart
spontaneously.

Lord, thank You for Your
Presence
which causes the spirit of praise;

and thank You for the
gift
of praise.
>>Amen.
>>
D. E. D.

35 Why Am I Sometimes Ungrateful? (1)

PRAISE FROM PROPHET

Really, they are without any
excuse.
Why?
>>They knew about God but
>>didn't respect Him as God;
>>Nor did they thank Him.
>>Actually, their thinking
>>became an exercise in
>>futility,
>>and senseless thinking is
>>darkened thinking,
>>>isn't it?

PRAISE BY PEN

One reason for thanklessness to
God
is this second-cause kind of thinking.
    You know, tracing your blessings
    to something other than the
    Primary Source.

Well, now, let's dig into this.
    For starters, our vision is usually
    myopic.
        What is near and immediate—
        that's what we look at
        rather than catching sight
        of the long view.
So, something good happens to us.
That something good appears to be the
fruit
of hard work,
of prudence,
of exertion, or
of friends' kindnesses.
    How natural to focus our
    gratitude
    on things like these
    and these alone.
    After all, these kinds of things appear to
    be the cause.
    The real fact?
        The Original Mover,
        The First Cause,
        The Being of beings—He is the
        One to whom our
        thanks
        are chiefly due.

Here is an analogy:
    I want to help a friend.
    I can help him best
    by persuading a third
    person
    to do something nice.

> Settled, the third
> person does his thing.
> Now, to whom is my friend
> really indebted?
>> To me?
>> Or to the third person?
> Certainly my friend will
> say "thank you"
> to the third person;
>> but the plain truth
>> is just this: I am
>> the principal actor,
>> the "grand mover,"
>> the author of the kindness.
> Simply because a third person
> was involved
> does not mean my
> kindness
> was in any way diminished.

But here's the catch:
> While it is easy enough
> to see the point
> in the analogy,
>> it seems terribly hard
>> to apply it
>> to God.
>> The plain fact is that
>> often we get food and
>> clothes
>> by our own hard work
>> but assign nothing to
>> the ample Hand of
>> God.

>> John Venn, *Sermons*, Volume 1

John Venn (1759-1813) played an important role on the "evangelical team" in the England of his day. He helped to fight slavery, was a founder of a pioneering missionary society, and an effective preacher.

PRAISE THROUGH PRAYER

Lord, Your steady love
just won't quit,
    it won't quit for
    those
    who honor and respect
    You.
Your goodness goes right on
to my children's children,
    to all who keep Your laws
    and remember to obey Your
    commandments.
              Psalm 103:17-18

36   Why Am I Sometimes Ungrateful? (2)

PRAISE FROM PROPHET

O God, right out of
Your goodness
You provided for the
needy.
              Psalm 68:10b

PRAISE BY PEN

Now, there's a second reason
for our ungratefulness.

It's this: we have a
defective
view of
Providence.
    True, we feel grateful
    to God
    when Providence is
    obvious,
    such as remarkable
    deliverance or
    unusual success.

But how sad!
Even when we admit
Providence in one event
we generally say,
"Providence had nothing
to do with some other
good things that happened."
The fact?
God does not work in
some things
more than in
others.
True, He lets us *in*
on His involvement
in some things more than
in others.
Reason? So we
can "catch on" to
what He is doing in
everything.

Sometimes He doesn't
use any instrument at
all
in order to show us that
when He does use an
instrument
He's still the One
doing the business!
Well, far be it from me
to check someone else's
emotional temperature
when he
experiences God-actually-
and-obviously-involved.
But I must say this much:
The very reason God sometimes
lets us in on how He works
proves our limited understanding,
our imperfect picture of God-at-work.

You know, if we could see
God-at-work
as He is seen in

heaven,
we would see God involved
in one place or happening
just as He is in every
other! Even in the details!
   He is not "there"
   sometimes, and
   absent other times.
   What "stands out"
   to us
   is regular to Him.
   He is always employed!
      The God of Israel never
      goes to sleep.
               John Venn, *Sermons*, Vol. 1

PRAISE THROUGH PRAYER

No earthly father loves like You,
No mother, half so mild,
Bears and forbears as You have done
With me Your sinful child.
               Frederick W. Faber

Frederick W. Faber (1814-1863) was ordained in the Church of England in 1839. He became an enthusiastic follower of John Henry Newman at Oxford. After having spent several years on the Continent studying Roman Catholicism, he was reordained as a Roman Catholic priest in 1847. He is best remembered as the writer of 150 hymns.

---

37   Be Glad, Sing, and Dance for Joy!

PRAISE FROM PROPHET

Life was in Him!
That life was the
light
men live by.
          John 1:4

PRAISE BY PEN

Evangelion is the Greek
word
for "Gospel."
What does it mean?
    It means
        good,
        merry,
        glad,
        joyful news.
    It means the kind of
        news
        that makes a man's
        heart glad,
        that makes him
        sing,
        dance,
        leap for joy,
as when David
killed
Goliath the giant.
The Jews got good news
that day!
Their fearful, cruel
enemy
was finished!
They were delivered from
danger,
all of it!
No wonder they were so glad
they
        sang,
        danced,
        were joyful.
So it is that the
Evangelion
of God (the "Gospel,"
the "New Testament")
is joyful news
    with a good hearing

around the world,
> for it tells us about
> Christ
> the perfect "David,"
> who fought sin and
> death,
> and who fought the devil
> too,
> and won!

Now, do you see what this means?
> All men in jail to
> > sin,
> all men wounded by
> > death,
> all men overcome by the
> > devil,
> —all such men are,
> neither by merit nor
> because they deserve it,
> > loosed!
> > made right!
> > restored to life!
> > saved!
> > given their freedom!
> > brought into God's favor!
> > put in harmony with God!

All that is great news,
and as many as believe it,
> sing,
> praise, and
> thank God—
well! they just can't
help but be glad,
> sing,
> > dance for joy.

William Tyndale, A Pathway unto The Holy Scripture

William Tyndale (c. 1494-1536), influenced by the works of Erasmus and Luther, was determined to give the common people the Bible in their own language. Not at liberty to work in England, he printed his English New Testament in Germany. Mistakenly believing it was safe for him to come out of hiding, he settled in Antwerp, Belgium, where he was arrested, tried and convicted of heresy. He was burned at the stake on October 6, 1536.

PRAISE THROUGH PRAYER

You, God, are
   my Love,
   the Life of all souls,
   the Life of lives,
   Livingness itself.

You, God, will
   never change.
God! You are the
   Life of my soul.
St. Augustine, Confessions

38 Laughter and Cheer

PRAISE FROM PROPHET

What is the secret of a
happy face?
   A glad heart.
What causes a broken spirit?
   Sorrow in your heart.
Proverbs 15:13

PRAISE BY PEN

I shall face life
cheerfully
and with anticipation.
I shall learn to
laugh,
even at myself.
    "A merry heart does you
    good—like medicine;
    but a broken spirit
    dries up
    your bones."
    The Bible also says,
    "Your strength comes from
    quiet faith."
    Listen once more:
    "Throw all your anxieties
    onto Jesus;
    He really cares for you."

I know that Elsie Robinson
is right
when she says,
    "Unpleasantness can be a
    disease.
    It provides an escape for
    our cowardice,
    an excuse for our
    laziness,
    an alibi for our
    cussedness, and
    a spotlight for our
    conceit."

I shall therefore do as
Muriel Lester
suggests:
    "Hunt for self-pity as
    you would hunt for
    lice"—
    and loathe it with the same
    loathing.

I shall keep my
capacity to laugh,
even at myself.
> When I get tense and take
> myself
> too seriously,
> I shall deliberately
> walk to the looking glass and
> burst out laughing.
> Even if I do not feel like
> laughing
> when I go,
> I feel more like it when
> I see the man in the glass
> laughing.

"You will never break
down,"
said a doctor to a friend of
mine,
"for you have a hair-trigger
laugh."

          E. Stanley Jones, *Abundant Living*, Week 13, Saturday

---

E. Stanley Jones, (d. 1970s) known affectionately to thousands as "Brother Stanley," served as a most effective evangelist for more than fifty years.

PRAISE THROUGH PRAYER

Confident God,
> going steadily on
> amid the deflections and
> betrayals of men,
> help me to have Your
> patience and

Your confidence.
From now on, God,
> I am eternally
> linked
> with You.

When You fall
I fall;
    until then
    I stand.
    Praise God!
    Amen.

                E. Stanley Jones, *Abundant Living*, Week 13, Saturday

CHAPTER SIX

Victory! Deliverance!

When we
bless God
for mercies
we prolong them.
When we
bless Him
for miseries
we usually
end them.

              Charles H. Spurgeon

Spurgeon (1834-1892), English Baptist preacher, possessed powerful gifts of oratory. By the age of twenty-two he had become the most popular preacher in England. The Metropolitan Tabernacle, seating 6,000, was opened in London in 1861. He served there until his death. During his lifetime over 2,000 sermons and forty-nine volumes of commentaries and devotions written by Spurgeon were published.

---

39 God Protects Me

PRAISE FROM PROPHET

In trouble?
Never mind.
   I will be with you.
   I will rescue you.
   I will honor you.
                         Psalm 91:15b

PRAISE BY PEN

Years ago I lived
near the Rhine River.
   The river there is
   wider than the Thames River
   at London Bridge,
      and also extremely rapid.

Well, being a practiced swimmer
I had no hesitation taking a
dip
whenever I wished.
   I was, however, always
   careful
   to stay near the shore
   so the current would have
   no chance to carry me
   away.

But once I was a bit careless.
   It happened unconsciously.
   But there I was! In mid-
   stream.
   Rough? Extremely.
   The water rushed along
   like a galloping horse.
      I tried to swim against
      the tide.

                No luck.
                Then! Before I could say,
                "Jack Robinson,"
                I found myself far from
                home.
                Almost tired out,
                I floated on my back,
                got a bit of rest,
                then looked around for a
                landing place,
                because by this time it
                was either "sink or swim."
With much difficulty
I got near shore,
but the rocks were
ragged and sharp;
I simply couldn't
walk ashore
or I would be torn to
bits.
I had but one alternative:
     to return to mid-stream.
By this time I gave up
all hope.
But! Then! A sight
     for sore eyes:
     A perfect creek was
     coming up!
     It was smooth, and
     I could land.
     Carried violently by
     the swift current, I
actually managed to
get into that creek.
                But the story is by
                no means finished:
                There stood a building
                (then I knew nothing
                about it; later I found
                out it was a powder mill).
                The last thing I remember
                was striking my head

against
one of the piles on which the
building stood.
Unconscious, I knew nothing
until I hit shore on the
other side
of the mill.

Coming to,
I found myself in a
calm
safe
place,
perfectly well,
without even soreness or
weariness!
Everything was ok
except
    the distance of my
    clothes—five miles!
A crowd had gathered on
shore
by this time;
One gentleman in
particular
had something to say:
"I saw you go under the
    mill,
and I saw when you came
    up
on the other side of the
    mill.
    You were twenty minutes
    under the building!"

        John Fletcher, quoted by John Wesley, *A Short Account of the Life and Death of The Rev. John Fletcher.*

John William Fletcher (1729-1785), born in Switzerland, came into contact with Methodism while working as a tutor in England. In 1760 he became vicar of Madeley, a rough mining town. Most of his writings were directed against Calvinism in defense of Wesleyan doctrines.

PRAISE THROUGH PRAYER

Lord, You are
   My Protector,
   My Shelter,
   My God.
   In You I trust.
      Amen.
                Psalm 91:2

40   God Is with Me in My Temptations

PRAISE FROM PROPHET

Who is the Lord good to?
   To those who wait for
   Him;
   To those who seek
   Him.
What is a good attitude?
   To wait quietly
   for God to
   rescue
   you.
                Lamentations 3:25-26

PRAISE BY PEN

This may happen
now that you are
a-Christian-who-means-business:
   Storms—big ones!
   Temptations, too.
   You could feel
   you have
   nothing,
      neither common grace nor
         special grace.

Don't be afraid
even if it seems
you
have good
reason
to be afraid.
 Instead,
 have a "lover's faith"
 in our Lord;
 He isn't far,
 even if you can't
 feel His
 love
 just now.
He will keep an eye on
you.
He may give you the
sense
of His Presence very
soon,
 this time with a more
 burning
 moving
 of His grace
 than you have ever
 felt before.
  Then! you will be
  healed again,
  totally restored.
But this is only for
a while,
 for all at once
 you will feel
 helpless
 again, barren,
 battered in your boat,
 tossed now here,
  now there,
  never knowing where you
  are
  or where you are going.
Still do not despair;
He will come!

He will come very soon!
I promise you that.
    He will come in His
    own time
    to relieve you,
    to do radical surgery
    that will relieve all
      misery—
far better relief
than ever before!
Now, even after that,
suppose you were to be left
alone again.
Well, just hang in there
quietly;
He will come again.
    If you will endure
    His absences
    with patient humility,
    He will return
    more gloriously,
    more joyfully
    than before.
Why all this back and forth
business?
    Because He is fitting
      you
      to His will,
    as your leather glove
      fits your
      hand.

The Book of Privy Counsel

The Book of Privy Counsel was written by the unknown author of *The Cloud of Unknowing,* a devotional masterpiece from medieval England.

PRAISE THROUGH PRAYER

Lord, You have made
known

to me
the way life works;
> You fill me,
> right up to the
> brim,
> with Your Presence.
>> Amen.
>>> Acts 2:28

41 One Way God Develops Patience in Me

PRAISE FROM PROPHET

It is the Lord you must
wait for:
> With Him comes strength;
> with Him comes courage.

So you see why you must
wait for the Lord.
>> Psalm 27:14

PRAISE BY PEN

Well, since God seems to
go away,
then return—
> in that double action
> He doubly tests us
> in secret
> to get His work done
> in us.

When your fervor is gone—
which seems to you as if *He*
is gone—
> though this is not so—

He is in fact testing your
patience.
> You should know this:
> When God withdraws the

sense
of His Presence,
with its sweetness,
    its feelings,
    its flaming desires,
still! He never—but never!—
withdraws His grace
from His
chosen children.
You see, I just can't
believe
He would ever take away His
special grace
from His
chosen children
who have once been
touched
by it,
    unless, of course,
    one has committed
    "mortal sin."
You see, these sensory
things: sweetness,
    fervent feelings,
    flaming desires—
well, these are not in
themselves
grace, just signs of
grace.
    Often they are withdrawn
    to test our
    patience,
    and often we get
    many other
    spiritual benefits too.
   —More than we think!
Realize this:
Grace itself is
    so exalted,
    so pure,
    so spiritual
that, really, it cannot
be felt by our senses.

True, the signs can be
felt,
but not grace itself.

So you see why our Lord
sometimes withdraws the
signs—
    He does it to increase
    your patience, and to
    test your patience
        and not for this reason
        only
        but for many others
        which I won't discuss
        here.
The Book of Privy Counsel

PRAISE THROUGH PRAYER

Yes, Lord, You are my
rock, and my
fortress.
    For Your sake
    lead me,
    guide me.
    Also rescue me
    from the hidden
    trap.
        You are my
        protection.
Amen.
Psalm 31:3-4

42   My Foes and Fears Defeated in Christ!

PRAISE FROM PROPHET

Don't be afraid;
    I am with you.
Don't be dismayed;

I am your God.
What will I do for
you?
    I will put steel in you,
    give you real help,
    uphold you with
        my
        victorious
        right
        hand.
                Isaiah 41:10

PRAISE BY PEN

Remember: every fear,
    every trouble,
    every sickness,
    every sin you may face
        —all this has been and is
        overcome
        by the One you follow—
        Christ.
When fears,
    sickness,
    sins
    threaten to overwhelm you,
    and to beat you into submission
    by their very overbearing
    presence,
    just calmly look
    each one
    in the eye
    and say,
        "I am not afraid of
        you.
        You have been and are
        decisively
        beaten by my Lord.
        Will you bend your neck?
        There,

      I knew it!
      The footprint of the Son of
      God
      is upon your neck."
This confidence is your starting point:
    Nothing can touch you
    that hasn't touched
    Him,
    and that hasn't been
    defeated
    by Him;
    and if you open
    your life
    to His power,
    every ill
    can be defeated
    again by you through His
    grace.
    You
        need
        not
        be
        defeated
        by
        anything
unless you consent to be.
    If you throw your will
    on the side of
    victory,
        then the whole of
        the Universe of Reality
        throws itself
        behind your will,
        releases it,
        reinforces it,
        redeems it—
        and you!
    You are caught up in a
    tide of victory,
    and nothing—but nothing!—
    can stop it

except your refusal to
cooperate.

Paul could say,
"I do not frustrate
the grace of God"—
   "I do not block its
   redemption,
   nor frustrate its healing
   purposes."
Therefore,
an Almighty Will
worked within his
will,
and he arose a rhythmical,
   harmonious,
   adequate person.

You can be the same.
        E. Stanley Jones, *Abundant Living*, Week 11,
        Tuesday

PRAISE THROUGH PRAYER

Why do I say "thank you"
to God
with all my heart?
   Why, because He gives me
   victory
   by the power of my
   Lord,
   Jesus Christ.
      Amen and Amen.
            I Corinthians 15:57

43 Be Happy! Someone Has Found God

PRAISE FROM PROPHET

When he finally
gets

> back
>   home,
> he invites his
> friends and neighbors
> in for a house
> party.
>   "Look!" he says
>   with great excitement,
>   "I have found the
>   sheep—
> You know, the one that was
> lost."
>   Luke 15:6

PRAISE BY PEN

Oh, Good God!
what happens in a
man
    to make him rejoice
    more at the salvation
    of a person
    who was given
        up for lost,
        then delivered
        from greater danger,
    than over a person
    who has never lost
    hope,
        or never been in real
        danger?

It appears, Lord, that
You
react just as we do,
because You once said,
Merciful Father, that
    You "rejoice more over
        one who repents than
        over ninety-nine
        good people who

need no repentance."
We listen with a lot of
excitement
when we hear how
the lost sheep
is brought home again
on the shepherd's
shoulders
> while the angels get
> happy.

We have the same reaction
when lost money is
found
and put back in its
place,
> and the neighbors
> get happy
> with the woman who
> found it.

What joy!
> What festivity!
>> Yes! in Your house.
>> We want to cry
>> when such stories
>> are read in Your
>> house.
> For example: the
> younger son
> who was dead and
> came alive
> again!
> The lost was
> found!

You get very happy, Lord,
and express Your joy
through us, and
through Your angels,
> who are holy
> because, in love,
> You share Your
> holiness with them.

You are always the same,
Lord,
   and You can see how
   the whole puzzle
   is going to look
     when it's all
     together.
>St. Augustine, *Confessions*, Book 8, Chapter III

PRAISE THROUGH PRAYER

Lord, the clue to Your
mercy
in Jesus is simple
   and
   beautiful:
     You allow Yourself
     to be lost
     only where You
     can be
     found.
Amen.
>Walter Hilton, *The Scale of Perfection*

44   The Salvation of Our Children

PRAISE FROM PROPHET

Our faith is in God Himself.
Why?
   Because His power is
   at work
   in us;
   Because He is quite
   prepared
   to do far more
   than we can even

> ask
> or
> think!
>
> Ephesians 3:20

PRAISE BY PEN

The young Augustine had lived a life characterized by doubts, mistresses, and self-centeredness. For many years his mother daily prayed and pleaded with God to save Augustine's soul, all to no avail—so it seemed. Then it happened! He came under the influence of Bishop Ambrose of Milan and at the age of thirty-three Augustine was converted. His friend Alypius was a witness to the conversion. This is the final, deeply moving paragraph of his conversion story.

After my conversion
    Alypius and I went to
    mother
    and told her what
    happened.
        You can imagine
        her great joy!
We explained to her
how it took place.
    She jumped up
    and threw her
    arms around me!
    She prayed a prayer of
    deep gratitude
    to God who is
    "able to do exceedingly
    abundantly
    above all we
    ask
    or
    think."
She saw that God
had answered her
prayer
very much more
than she had ever
asked

>through all her
>tears
>and
>sobs.

Lord, what evidence that You
had in fact answered
prayer at that
deeper level!

>You converted me so
>thoroughly
>that I didn't even
>look for a wife,
>much less find more
>girl friends;
>In fact, Lord, You
>took all real "worldly"
>desires right out of
>my mind and heart!

>You gave me the ability
>to let my weight down
>100% on faith in Jesus
>Christ—that's what
>mother dreamed for me
>years ago!

>>So it was that You, Lord,
>>turned mother's grief
>>into joy
>>greater than she had
>>ventured even to desire,
>>and greater, too, than the
>>cherished wish she had had
>>many years ago
>>of having grandchildren.

St. Augustine, *Confessions*, Book 8, Chapter XII

St. Augustine (354-430), bishop of Hippo, was the most important of the early Church Fathers. As a champion of orthodoxy he has had enormous influence on the Christian world. Among his writings are *The City of God* and his autobiography, *Confessions*.

PRAISE THROUGH PRAYER

I give my praise and thanks
to the God
who sits on the Throne of
Heaven.
To Him go blessing,
    honor,
    glory,
    might for ever and ever!
Amen.
                Revelation 5:13b

45 Victory over Temptation

PRAISE FROM PROPHET

Because Jesus Himself
suffered and was
tempted,
    He can help
    us
    when we are tempted.
                Hebrews 2:18

PRAISE BY PEN

After I returned home
from the small group
meeting in
Aldersgate Street,
    the devil gave me a
    bad time,
    very bad!
I cried for help;
the temptations went
away.

They returned
not once, but many
times.
Just as often as they
came
I looked up for help, and
God "sent me help from His
home in heaven."
    Just here
    I discovered the
    difference
    between the converted
    life
    and the unconverted life.

    Before my conversion,
    I fought with all my
    might,
    but it was fighting to
    do things "just so";
    true, I had some measure of
    freedom,
    but only a measure.
        Uneven results!
        Sometimes I won,
        but usually I lost;
        Now! after my conversion,
        I always win. . . .

The very moment I woke up,
I prayed,
"Jesus! Master!"
    That prayer came from my
    lips
    but also from my
    heart.
        What a discovery!
        All my strength
        came
        by keeping my
        eyes
        on
        Jesus,

by waiting all the
time
on
Him.

I went to St. Paul's
Cathedral
in the afternoon;
there I tasted the
good
Word of God
in the anthem by the
choir:
"My song shall be
always
of the lovingkindness
of the Lord:
with my mouth
will I ever be
showing
forth thy truth
from one generation to
another."

But! The enemy injected
a fear
even in that setting:
"If you really believe,
why can't you see more
changes
in yourself?"
Here was my answer (though
it was really the Spirit's answer):
"I don't know.
What I do know is this:
Now I have
peace
with
God.
I do not
sin
today.
Jesus, my Master,

tells me not
to be worried
about
tomorrow."
>John Wesley, *Journal*, May 24-25, 1738

PRAISE THROUGH PRAYER

Lord, You alone are
    good,
    just,
    holy;
You can do all things;
You can accomplish all things;
only the sinner You leave without
    help.
Amen.
>Thomas à Kempis, *Of the Imitation of Christ*, Book III, Chapter III, 5

46 Great Is Thy Faithfulness

PRAISE FROM PROPHET

God in heaven:
    I am going to lift my
    heart
    up to You;
    I am going to lift my
    hands
    up to You.
>Lamentations 3:41

PRAISE BY PEN

I feel like somebody
did me dirt;
I am depressed:
    My teeth are grinding

on gravel,
I am cowering
in ashes.
I have no peace.
Happiness? I've forgotten
what it's like.
Anybody can see why I say,
 "Gone is my honor;
 Gone is all hope."

Lord, don't forget me:
 I'm hurting.
 I'm as bitter as wormwood
 and gall.
 I'm stuck with my
 thoughts.
 I'm finished.

Ah! Hope at last—
I remembered something good:
 "The Lord's love
 goes on and on,
 The Lord's mercies
 don't quit,
 The Lord's mercies
 are new every single
 morning,
 'Great is Thy
 faithfulness.' "

Release! My soul sings,
 "The Lord takes
 care
 of me.
 That's why I
 hope
 in Him."

Yes, the Lord is good
to those who keep their
cool
and go to Him for
help.
How to handle depression?

>
> Here is advice as sound
> as a pre-inflation dollar:
> > "Wait quietly
> > for
> > God
> > to
> > come
> > and
> > help
> > you."
> > > Lamentations 3:16-26

PRAISE THROUGH PRAYER

> Lord, You came near
> to me
> when I asked You to.
> > You said, "Do not
> > fear!"
> > > Amen.
> > > > Lamentations 3:57

47 God Gives Me Faith

PRAISE FROM PROPHET

> The Gospel?
> > I'm proud of it,
> > never ashamed!
> Why?
> > It is God's power;
> > It is rescue;
> > It works for all
> > who have faith—
> > > it works for Jews,
> > > it works for everybody
> > > else too.
> > > > Romans 1:16

PRAISE BY PEN

> I'd be sunk—

really sunk—
what with temptations,
    tribulations,
    adversities.
They seem to come every
day!
    But I am not sunk
    because faith
        goes
        with
        me
        to
        deliver
        me.
We have God's promise,
you know,
that God will
        help us
        clothe us
        feed us
        fight for us
        get rid of enemies for us.
Now you see what is
meant
by the old saying,
    "The righteous live
    by faith";
    Indeed, they live
    "from faith to faith"—
        and by that last phrase
        we mean simply this:
        As soon as a Christian
        is delivered
        from one temptation
        he has another
        and he overcomes
        that one by
        faith
        too.
What does the Bible say?
    "The man who has his
    sin
    forgiven is

happy;
his sin is gone!
No longer does the
    Lord
    look on him as a
    lawbreaker."
> William Tyndale, *Justification by Faith*

PRAISE THROUGH PRAYER

Lord! You are blessed and glorious.
God! Your goodness and mercy
just won't quit.
We are just creatures;
    You made us;
        You take care of us;
        You keep us breathing;
    You often rescue us out of the
        jaws of death.
We give ourselves to you once more
(as best we know how)
to say "Thank You" and to
praise Your Name,
    because You hear us when we
    call
    in times of trouble,
    and You do not say "No"
    to our prayers
    said when we are
    caught in the crunch.
Lord, even when we said everything
was lost—
    our ship,
        our car, furniture, and things,
        even our lives—
    Well! Just then You
    were kind
    and rescued us out of
    bankruptcy.
Now, we are safe and sound;
How could we do less than say,
"Thank You"?

We honor Your holy Name
through Jesus Christ, our
Lord.
    Amen.

Book of Common Prayer (edition of Charles II, 1662)

48 God Gives Me Everything

PRAISE FROM PROPHET

Every good endowment,
every beautiful and perfect
gift—
    all of it comes from
    heaven,
    from the Father who
    gives light,
    the Father who is
    100% dependable,
    the Father who does not
    change.
                  James 1:17

PRAISE BY PEN

Here's a good idea:
    Make a habit of
    looking at all you
    get
    as gifts from God,
        undeserved but
        given just as often
        as we are in need and
        all due to His
        mercy.
God gives;
God may take away.
He gave
us
all we have:
    life
        health

reason
    enjoyment
    inner light.
Let's face it:
    Whatever is good and holy
    in us,
    Whatever faith we have,
    Whatever of a renewed will,
    Whatever love for God,
    Whatever power over ourselves,
    Whatever hope of heaven—
        He is responsible for all of
        it!
In fact, He gave us
    relatives,
    friends,
    education,
    training,
    knowledge,
    the Bible,
    the Church.
    Every bit comes from
    Him!
He gave;
He may take away.
While He continues His blessings,
    let's follow
        David
        and
        Jacob
        by living in constant
        praise
        and
        thanksgiving
        and offering to let
        Him
        have
        back
        whatever
        He
        has given
        us.

> John Henry Newman, *Parochial Sermons* (1842), Vol. 5

John Henry Newman (1801-1890), English cardinal, was ordained in the Anglican Church and adjudged one of the ablest preachers of Oxford. He helped organize the Oxford Movement and wrote tracts in defense of the Anglo-Catholic Movement. In 1845 he was received into the Roman Catholic Church. His most famous writings are *Apologia pro Vita Sua* (his religious autobiography) and the hymn "Lead, Kindly Light."

PRAISE THROUGH PRAYER

Lord, I have made a vow
to You,
a vow to say, "Thank
You."
   Amen.

                    Psalm 56:12

49   I Am Made for Faith and Not for Fear

PRAISE FROM PROPHET

Jesus' Name!
That's the Name to have
faith in.
   Do you see this man
   here?
   This man you see right
   now
   and know?
   He is now strong!
   Perfectly well!
      Faith in Jesus
      made him whole;
      he has perfect health
      and you see him with
      your very own
      eyes.
              Acts 3:16

PRAISE BY PEN

Fear is not my native land;
faith is.
I am so made that
    worry
    and
    anxiety
        are sand
        in the machinery
        of life;
        faith is oil.

I live better
by faith and confidence
than by fear and doubt and anxiety.
    In anxiety and worry
    my being
    is gasping for breath—
        these are not my native air.
    But in faith and confidence
    I breathe freely—
        these are my native air.

A John Hopkins doctor
says that
    "we do not know why
    it is that the worriers
    die sooner
    than the non-worriers,
        but that is a fact."

    But I, who am simple of
    mind,
    think I know:
        we are inwardly constructed,
        in nerve and tissue
        and brain cell and
        soul, for faith
        and not for fear.
        God made us that way.
        Therefore, the need of faith

is not something imposed on us
dogmatically,
but it is written in us
intrinsically.

> E. Stanley Jones, *Abundant Living*, Week 13, Sunday.

PRAISE THROUGH PRAYER

O God, my Creator,
I thank You
that faith is written on the
    heart of the universe
    and on my
    heart.

Thank You for the healing
that comes
just now
by the simple
recognition
of that fact.
    Thank You for the
    renewal
    of faith I sense.

Thank You that
healing
has gone into every
cell
of my body and
    every thought of my
    mind.

Praise to You,
    my Creator,
    my Re-creator.

    Amen
        D. E. D.

SOURCES

Anglican Hymn Book. London: Church Book Room Press Limited, 1965.

Basset, Elizabeth, *Love Is My Meaning: An Anthology of Assurance.* London: Darton, Longman and Todd Ltd., 1973; Atlanta: John Knox Press, 1974.

Book of Common Prayer. Several editions including the Prayer Book of Charles II, 1662.

The Book of Worship for Church and Home, with Orders of Worship, Services for the Administration of Sacraments, and Aids to Worship According to the Usages of the Methodist Church. Nashville: The Methodist Publishing Company, 1964.

Colledge, Eric, editor, *The Mediaeval Mystics of England.* London: John Murray, 1962.

Duffield, G. E., editor, *The Works of William Tyndale in the Courtenay Library of Reformation Classics.* Berkshire, England: The Sutton Courtenay Press, 1964.

Herbert, George, *Works,* F. E. Hutchinson, editor. Oxford: University Press, 1941.

Houghton, Frank, *Amy Carmichael of Dohnavur.* Fort Washington, Pa.: Christian Literature Crusade, n.d.

Johnson, Mauree, *Our God Is Beautiful.* Atlanta: Published by the author, n.d.

Jones, E. Stanley, *Abundant Living.* Nashville: Cokesbury, 1946.

Juliana of Norwich, *Revelations of Divine Love Recorded by Juliana, Anchoresss at Norwich, Anno Domini 1373,* Grace Warrack, editor. London: Methuen and Company, 1901.

Library of Christian Classics, Vols. VII, X. London: SCM, 1955, 1956.

March, W. W. S., *Ground of the Heart: A Commentary on the General Thanksgiving.* London: The Faith Press; New York: Morehouse-Barlow Co., Inc., 1963.

Murray, Andrew, *With Christ in the School of Prayer*. Old Tappan, N.J.: Fleming H. Revell Company, 1953.

Outler, Albert C., *A Library of Protestant Thought*. New York: Oxford University Press, 1964.

Robertson, J.D., *Minister's Worship Handbook*. Grand Rapids: Baker Book House, 1974.

Temple, William, *Readings in St. John's Gospel*. New York: Macmillan Co., 1947.

Thomas à Kempis, *Of the Imitation of Christ*. New York: Thomas Nelson and Sons Ltd., n.d.

Tozer, A. W., *God's Greatest Gift to Man*. Harrisburg, Pa.: Christian Publications, Inc., n.d.

Venn, John, *Sermons*, Vol. I, third edition. London: J. Hatchard and Rivingtons, 1818.

Wesley, John, *A Short Account of the Life and Death of the Rev. John Fletcher*. Halifax: W. Milner, Cheapside, 1851.

Williams, Charles, editor, *The Letters of Evelyn Underhill*. London: Longmans, Green and Co., 1943.

www.ingramcontent.com/pod-product-compliance
Lightning Source LLC
Chambersburg PA
CBHW070914160426
43193CB00011B/1453